THE MYSTERY OF SILENCE

Making Sense of Life When God Seems Absent

DAVID OLSHINE

ENDORSEMENTS

"Using his life as a springboard for exploration, David Olshine's *The Mystery of Silence* unfolds the divine silence. In a loud world, this is no easy feat. Olshine's memories, stories, and research weave together as a tool for those who hunger to 'be still and know that I am God.'"
—Laura Baber, author of *Rhythms of Restoration*

"*The Mystery of Silence* is a much-needed and restorative elixir for someone like me who actually *prefers* to be surrounded by noise and feels somewhat uncomfortable when things go silent. Heck, after the first chapter, I even took my earbuds out so I could read it meditatively."
—Rick Bundschuh, author, pastor of Kauai Christian Fellowship, and troublemaker, Kauai, Hawaii

"*The Mystery of Silence* is a breath of fresh air, as David Olshine writes with depth, authenticity, and wonderful relatable stories. You will grow in your faith and find hope on every page. Olshine is a masterful communicator who makes this book totally enjoyable to read."
—Jim Burns, president, Homeword, and best-selling author of *Doing Life with Your Adult Children: Keep Your Mouth Shut and the Welcome Mat Out*, Dana Point, California

"*The Mystery of Silence* is a must-read. David Olshine steps confidently, but with humility and transparency, into the discomfort of silence in the presence of God. For anyone looking for solace and guidance in the face of the unclear quiet, this book is for you."
—Dr. Anne Lord Bailey, endurance competitor, Team UNBROKEN on Amazon Prime's TV show *World's Toughest Race: Eco Challenge Fiji*, Asheville, North Carolina

"Most of our life with God is quiet. Too quiet sometimes. In *The Mystery of Silence*, David Olshine shares his soul—his experiences with pain, suffering, and doubt. He invites us to trust the silence we often perceive from God isn't something to dread, fear, or cause us to roll our eyes. It's something to lean into because even God's silence has plenty to say to us."

—Nick Cunningham, Lead Pastor, Emmaus Church, Irmo, South Carolina

"David Olshine's writing is raw, honest, and vulnerable. *The Mystery of Silence* escorts the reader beyond the buzz created by busyness and distraction, into a sanctuary in which, amidst the silence, we can actively hear God's voice."

—Samantha Evans; author of *The Rocky Path of Mourning: Navigating the Loss of a Loved One* and *Love Letters to Miscarriage Moms*

"David Olshine helped me understand my need to be more silent in order to grow in my relationship with God when facing a difficult journey. I appreciated his vulnerability to share his personal family struggles and his own doubts."

—Dr. Paul Marzhan, Lead Pastor of Crossroads Church, church planter, entrepreneur, and builder of sacred spaces, Minneapolis, Minnesota

"Sabbath, silence, and solitude. Three gifts God gives us that we all too frequently overlook or avoid! Dr. David Olshine invites us to reconsider these gifts as choices that can open up our world and faith to more fully experience a God who is for us, who loves us, and who comes alongside us, Emmanuel."

—Dr. Steve Moore, Executive Director, Murdock Foundation, Vancouver, Washington

"Greek philosopher Xenophanes once observed, 'If horses had gods, they would look like horses.' Interesting, isn't it, how so many who claim to be people of faith seem so determined to reduce mystery to something measurable? That's why my friend David Olshine's new book *The Mystery of Silence* is so important. We walk into the mystery of God; we do not define that mystery. So allow David Olshine to take you on a walk."

—Stuart Hall, Youth Communicator, author, director of ORANGE Student leadership and INFLUNSR. BigStuf Camps, Atlanta, Georgia

"I'm not sure a more practical and engaging book has ever been written on the subject of rest! We don't rest well. Dr. Olshine's topic, which seems antiquated by today's standards, teaches us about Sabbath and why we should implement and practice solitude and silence."

—Sugar Kyzer Jeffcoat, Family Director, Kittiwake Baptist Church, West Columbia, South Carolina

"As a family who is raising a young daughter with cystic fibrosis, I often wrestle with the mystery of silence that David Olshine explores in these pages. I often think of his example of faith and trust in God. No matter your circumstances, seasons of silence are unavoidable, and this book will be a tangible comfort and help for all who want to learn the practice of hearing God's voice."

—Wade Joye, Served 14 years as Worship Pastor at Elevation Church, Charlotte, North Carolina; Worship Consultant

"If your faith sometimes teeters on the precipice of doubt or you're straining to hear even a faint whisper from God in the midst of your struggle, this book is for you. David Olshine helps you listen beyond the silence to discover a profound and life-changing wonder you might never have otherwise heard."

—Drs. Les and Leslie Parrott, #1 New York Times best-selling authors of *Saving Your Marriage Before It Starts*, Seattle, Washington

"My friend and fellow teaching pastor David Olshine's newest book felt like it was written just for me. As a hyper-extrovert, I needed to be reminded of the importance of silence. This book is relational, practical, and biblical. The Olshine family journey offers a powerful illustration of faith as they faced adversity. The combination of mystery and silence offers a surprising path to the grace of God. Thank you for offering us directions."

—Dr. Jeff Philpott, author and Lead Pastor,
Sandhills Community Church, Columbia, South Carolina

"This book will be a refreshment to your soul. It's honest, thoughtful, and clearly forged in the furnace of David Olshine's experience and life. I love, that even with this heavy theme, I can still hear David's voice in this book—down-to-earth, humorous, and shaped by biblical truth. This book will provide help and hope to those who have experienced long nights when God does not seem to say a word."

—Duffy Robbins, Professor of Christian Ministries, youth ministry,
speaker, and author, Grove City College, Pennsylvania

"A wise mentor of mine once told me that 'God is always speaking, it's just that He sometimes speaks in silence.' Most of us are uneasy with the silence of God and need the wisdom and perspective of those who have walked with God through many different seasons of life. David Olshine, in *The Mystery of Silence*, is like a spiritual Sherpa, guiding the reader through many of life's most troubling challenges. Olshine speaks with fresh candor and personal vulnerability, resulting in a book that is both accessible and insightful."

—Dr. Timothy C. Tennent, president,
Asbury Theological Seminary; Wilmore, Kentucky

"I've known David Olshine and his family personally for twenty years. Reading his collection of life stories brought back memories of those challenging times for him and his family. For those who have not had the opportunity to watch and learn from these events like I have, I recommend this book. David's writing is refreshingly honest, heartfelt, and practical."

—Dr. Karen Grant, Professor of Youth Ministry, Family and
Culture, Columbia International University

"It's not the path that my husband and I planned on, but it's one that I feel blessed that God chose me for. As a mom of two incredible teenagers, one who just happens to have an autism diagnosis, it can be extremely hard to be still and quiet. David reminds us to be comfortable in the silence and draw near to God during that time. These words are so important for everyone; especially those caring for special-needs families."

—Michelle N. Hunt, Special Needs Coordinator, Mt. Horeb United Methodist Church, Lexington, South Carolina

"In this remarkable book, David Olshine invites us to find rest for our souls by embracing the mystery of silence: the silence that draws us into the depths of God; the silence that confronts us in times of doubt, anxiety, and grief; and the silence that renews our spirits. With uncommon warmth, humanity, wisdom, and humor, Olshine draws us into the experiences of silence that we often neglect or avoid. This is one of those rare books that combines deep reflection, rich expositions of biblical texts, and practical advice—made all the more relatable because Olshine shares much of his own personal journey."

—Dr. Daniel Hawk, professor of Old Testament and Hebrew, Ashland Theological Seminary, Ashland, Ohio

"Henri Nouwen said that 'spiritual maturity is a willingness to be led where you would rather not go.' Most people fight against being led into silence and solitude. David Olshine does an incredible job of leading us where we would rather not go. This book is an invitation into a space that God will bring transformation in your life."

—Brent Metcalf; Lead Pastor, Christ Church of the Valley, Cashiers, North Carolina

"David Olshine has written his most vulnerable work to date in *The Mystery of Silence*. From the moment I read the introduction, I was caught up in the journey of discovery. Masterful storytelling gives a glimpse into David's honest wrestle with a God who often meets us in silence. Olshine opens up the Scriptures in a way that brings light to the daily struggle I find myself in to trust God and quiet my heart. This is a must-read for any individuals who find themselves 'busy' in life or 'busy for God.'"

—Pastor Trevor Miller; Family Ministries Director, Mount Horeb Church, Lexington, South Carolina

"*The Mystery of Silence* presents one of God's greatest venues for communicating with the human soul. Sitting before Jesus to listen and learn will present each reader the opportunity to go deeper spiritually. While I experienced suffering numerous times over the years, God used silence to reach me on many levels. Doc Olshine is opening a treasure trove of truth for an overwhelmingly busy society. Read it and grow."
—**Dr. Mark Smith, president, Columbia International University, South Carolina**

"David Olshine's magnificent book is prophetically loud and clear book about silence—and its central role in following Jesus. As has often been said, the most used part of the body of Christ in the twenty-first century Western church has been the mouth; the ears have gone entirely unused. This jarring book invites the reader to embrace, once again, the sacred, holy, and ancient way of quiet in a world of frantic insanity. Find a quiet place and dig in."
—**A. J. Swoboda, professor of Bible, Theology, and World Christianity, Bushnell University; author of *Subversive Sabbath* and *After Doubt*, Portland, Oregon**

"A most timely work in the midst of global pandemics, environmental disasters, and rancorous political and religious divisions. David Olshine challenges us to ask questions of God that we all have from his own deep personal experience. Pick up this book!"
—**Michael Slaughter, Chief Strategist, Passionate Churches LLC, Cincinnati, Ohio**

"David Olshine's *The Mystery of Silence* masterfully addresses a subject that few people have dared to tackle and shares, through his own experience and the truths of Scripture, how to experience God's comfort and presence in those silent moments."
—**Laura Story, Grammy Award-winning artist; best hit *Blessings*; author of *I Give Up: When God Doesn't Fix It* and *So Long, Normal*, Atlanta, Georgia**

"*The Mystery of Silence* is really good stuff. It's a bases-loaded grand slam in the bottom of the ninth during the World Series kind of book. David Olshine's openness, humor, and practical insight will woo you into the story and help you understand your own."

—Dr. Larry Wagner, professor of Clinical Counseling; author of
Help Me Help Others

"In a loud and busy world where people are drained, divided, and distracted, silence is often ignored and unappreciated. I have rarely heard anyone in the church put an emphasis on silence. I know Dr. David Olshine, and as my brother and one I look up to, he has not only encouraged me to be silent before the Lord, he also practices it himself. If you need salve for the soul, please read *The Mystery of Silence* today. You will experience the love and power of God in an amazing way."

—Dr. Malcolm Walls, Pastor of Outreach and Next Steps, Sandhills Community Church, Columbia, South Carolina

The Mystery of Silence: Making Sense of Life When God Seems Absent
by Dr. David Olshine

TABLE OF CONTENTS

THE RUDE AWAKENING

"Silence isn't empty, it's full of answers."
—Unknown

I will never forget one defining moment my last year of graduate school. I was required to have a clinical education experience in a hospital setting. When I arrived at the local medical center, I was asked to serve on the oncology floor.

Five days a week during the month of January, from 8:00 a.m. to 5:00 p.m., I served as Assistant Chaplain. I would roam from room to room, talk, listen, and pray with patients. It was a very difficult and emotional place to work, and on a number of evenings, I would drive back home crying for the people I had met that day.

I saw five-year-old children, teenagers, moms, dads, young people, singles, elderly people, couples, wealthy people, and poor people—all battling cancer. All these folks were fighting for their lives. Cancer was no respecter of persons, religion, ethnicity, or birthplace.

One morning, I arrived a few minutes early, and I was checking in at the nurses' station. The attending nurse said, "Mr. Olshine, in room sixteen, Mr. Stone is having a bad day. Please don't see him if you want your life spared. He is in an awful mood. Downright mean."

Saying that to me is like telling a high school boy not to go into the girls' area at camp or not to stay out too late with your parents' car. I am a naturally born limits challenger (to some extent, aren't we all?).

I am a bit rebellious, curious, inquisitive, and have been told that I ask way too many questions. I push the bounds of a limit. I can't resist the opportunity. I test the elasticity, and then I go a little bit further. It either breaks and reveals new limits or snaps back and smacks me. So I had a brief discussion with the nurse.

"What is wrong with Mr. Stone?" I asked.

"He's having a tough time today," Nurse Thomas said.

"How so?"

"His cancer has spread to his lymph nodes and other places in his body. He feels very sick, is sleeping a lot, and is angry at the world."

I let most of the day go by because I wanted to give Mr. Stone some space.

Around 4:00 p.m., I decided to brace myself and venture into his room. I knocked and quietly entered. He was awake, alert, and staring out the window. He looked jaundiced.

"Hello, Mr. Stone, I am David Olshine. I am in graduate school and serve here as one of the chaplains. How are you today?"

Dumb question.

Silence.

I was twenty-three years old at the time and had never been in this situation before. I was a young buck with a theology degree almost in hand, sitting with a fifty-six-year-old man dying in a hospital bed. I did not know what to do. I did not know what to say.

"How are you feeling today?" I asked.

Another dumb question.

The room remained painfully silent, and I felt increasingly awkward.

Next up: My "A" game. It had worked for me dozens of times before, so I figured it would be fail-safe! This includes talking when I am in an unsettling environment, and I yap for a while.

Poor decision.

I like to talk. It helps me feel in control of my environment. I told Mr. Stone a few stories about me. He continued to gaze out the window. Mr. Stone had nothing to say. I was not sure if he was even listening. Next up, I shared a humorous story about me as a little kid. At least, I thought it was funny! When I hit the punchline, and I chuckled, his face remained as cold as ice.

He was not laughing. Awkward, persistent silence. I proceeded to start into another short monologue when Mr. Stone interrupted me.

"*Shut the hell up,*" he said.

I gazed at him and responded sheepishly, "Yes, sir."

Mr. Stone added with emphasis: "Stop talkin'."

"Okay."

I sat quietly, *not wanting* to say one word. He might bite my head off. He was in emotional and physical pain. He knew his fate. It was imminent. We sat together in uneasy silence. The discomfort level was extremely high for me. I looked at Mr. Stone, glanced at the floor, and stared at the muted television.

It felt like an hour of stillness, and inside, I wanted to run and hide. But I stayed. Fifteen minutes of unmitigated silence must have passed. Guess what: *Silence has a way of forging new beginnings.* Then Mr. Stone actually helped me relax.

"Hold my hand," he said unexpectedly.

I thought, *Wait… What? Really?*

I reached out and grabbed his rough skin. We sat together in silence for another ten minutes or so, again, both of us saying nothing.

I wouldn't dare!

Mr. Stone, a farmer from rural Kentucky, began to cry. My eyes started to get moist, too. And my hands were *sweating.* We had been holding hands for so long!

Mr. Stone finally spoke: "I am scared. I am going to die."

I looked into his eyes as gently as I could.

"My wife left me years ago," he continued. "My only son hates me. He blames me for the divorce. I am all by myself."

I nodded, sadly, letting him know I was with him.

Moments of silence. Then, to my surprise. Mr. Stone asked, "Would you pray for me? I need strength."

"Absolutely," I said. We prayed.

That day, I learned that silence is to be honored. I was humbled in that hospital room, almost humiliated in the sense that I almost blew a golden opportunity to listen well to another human being. I was seconds away from totally missing out on why silence is not only uncomfortable for me but necessary to get into my soul.

Silence was disconcerting and powerful. Silence was holy, and God was present. I needed to pay attention to the tension of silence.

A Lesson to Embrace

My time with Mr. Stone put me on an expedition of silence.

Silence is sacred, and in the grand scheme of things, I was learning how much I didn't know or like silence. I was on a new journey, a time of discovery that would later impact my life, my family, and my work. In fact, it would influence my whole worldview.

Anyone who knows me recognizes that I am not naturally a quiet person. I like to talk. In fact, I am paid to speak. I am a professor and a public communicator. *A professional at talking!*

It's not that I don't like to listen—I do. I love hearing people's stories. But talking comes naturally to me. Silence doesn't.

I really enjoy people and feed off the energy of being around them. My mom says that since I was a little kid, I have never known a stranger.

Let's talk about *silence* and *noise*.

First, let's get out of the way what this book is *not* about. This book is *not* extolling the virtues of introversion, nor is it about reprimanding the talkative tendencies of extraverts. This is *not* a book about the Myers-Briggs inventory or the Enneagram.

It is true that most of my introverted friends do quite well with silence, especially when the crowd gets larger. Introverts (I's) are inner-world people and need time to internally process before they explain what they are thinking and feeling. It's usually accurate that extroverts (E's) struggle with handling quiet and silence.

Most E's are external processors. I'm one of them.

Extroverts have the need to talk out loud, not just because they like to hear their voices, but because it's how extroverts process life. Extroverts talk *before* they think and *while* they think. But this book is not about the differences between extroverts and introverts.

The Mystery of Silence deals with why many people choose noise over silence, why some do not like silence, and how to deal with life when we feel God is silent. It is about how silence can enhance and reframe our interpersonal and intrapersonal skills and our emotional and spiritual lives. Countless people are uncomfortable with silence, especially when placed in situations in which friends and families have just experienced traumatic experiences of loss or death.

This book is about new ways to encounter silence.

Silence Has Much to Teach Us

We do not have to be afraid of silence, for it has the power to *transform* all of us. I have friends who love silence, and I admire them for it, but enjoying silence has not been my normative experience. When it comes to silence, I have never been a big fan. I like noise.

I told a number of people I was writing a book dealing with silence, and I heard all kinds of jokes related to the subject from my friends: "Of all people, *you* are writing a book on silence?" "What's it going to be, a hundred and fifty pages that are *blank*?" "How can anyone like you who has a bit of an attention deficit *even* consider silence?"

Valid points.

Don't we all want noise sometimes, really? Aren't we all a little distracted in today's world?

And even though silence has felt like a stranger, it has an intriguing power to be my friend. It has gotten my attention many times. Silence may mess with you. It certainly has been disturbing to me. What would have happened if Mr. Stone had never asked me to stop talking? I would have rambled on and on. We probably would have never enjoyed that sacred connection.

I am forever grateful for that encounter with him.

We can all feel intimidated when it comes to silence, discouraged when we do not know what to say, and mystified when we want God to speak and we feel He is all too quiet.

In this book, I identify some myths and misconceptions about the nature of silence and God's silence. I would like to reframe our view of silence so it creates wonder and astonishment in our souls.

Silence is not to be ignored. It has a message for all of us.

PART ONE

WRESTLING WITH SILENCE: WHY WE DISLIKE IT, WHY WE NEED IT

"You have a grand gift for silence, Watson.
It makes you quite invaluable as a companion."
—Arthur Conan Doyle, *The Complete Sherlock Holmes*

T*he Mystery of Silence* is a practical, pragmatic, yet intuitive and experiential look at why silence is not only powerful but is a mystery to be embraced as it relates to personal relationships with people and God. This book is *not* a scientific look at silence, nor is it about the science of mysteries.

In Part 1, we address some tough issues and questions about silence:

- What if silence has a mystical power that God wants us to tap into rather than be afraid of?
- What if noise is the actual enemy when it comes to truly knowing myself and God?
- What if God is more present in his silence than we may know?
- How does God use hardships to pull us into his world of silence?
- What are some practical ways to embrace silence?
- How do we make sense out of life when God seems absent?

The mystery of silence has guided my family and me. And hopefully it will guide you and yours as well.

CHAPTER ONE

DEAFENING SILENCE: FIFTEEN YEARS OF WAITING

"Silence is so freaking loud."
—Sarah Dessen

My wife, Rhonda, and I were married on a hot August day in Ohio. She was twenty-four years old, and I was twenty-six. We had dreams of changing the world together. Our first two years of married life were at times magical, wishing some of these experiences and moments could be bottled and savored. At other times, married life was smooth sailing, with some occasional hurdles, normal spats, and a few bumps in the road. Vocationally, we both served at the same local church. I was the youth pastor, and Rhonda was the director of Christian Education.

No matter what age or stage you're in, whether you are married, single, divorced, or widowed, life has a way of coming at us with great velocity. My wife and I have a story, and you have one. Our story will be different than yours, but they may have some common denominators. Perhaps you will resonate with some of the joys, jolts, and struggles that Rhonda and I identify in this book, and one day, you may find yourself or someone you love in similar shoes. Just when you think life couldn't get any better (or worse), stuff happens.

Once we had been married for two years, everything was about to change dramatically.

My wife *contracted* pregnancy! The following September, we were gifted with a beautiful, brown-eyed girl. We named her Rachel, meaning "little lamb." This name was a high compliment in biblical times—plus, we loved the name. Rachel was a great firstborn—she even slept through most of the nights! It was an awesome time for our family. Both our parents lived in the same city we did, so we had the chance to hang out with them quite often and gain some free grandparent babysitting.

About the time Rachel turned two years old, Rhonda and I started thinking about having another baby.

We began the *experiment!*

After about a year or so of trying to get pregnant, and being unsuccessful, we wondered if there might be a problem, so we sought medical advice. We visited a few specialists in Cincinnati and eventually came to the painful decision to start fertility treatment. We took the medication as prescribed. For more than a year, we worked on conceiving. Kept trying.

Nothing. No miracle, sign, or wonder.

Silence.

We prayed. We were on everyone's prayer list to have another baby. *Where is God?* I was thinking.

I was in the prime of my early thirties and had the honor and privilege of speaking at youth conferences, parent seminars, and youth worker venues regularly around the country. Even still, the "man of faith and power" and his wife could not conceive. It was breaking our hearts because it seemed like all our friends could wave a magic wand and become pregnant.

But not us.

Then one afternoon, my mother-in-law told us about a medical specialist in our city who had been a guest on the *Oprah* show. It took us several months to get in, but I must admit, the doctor was very impressive. I felt like, in twenty minutes, I learned everything there was to know about pregnancy and the science behind it. It was astounding. I did not really want more knowledge of our situation; I wanted a diagnosis and solution.

The doctor gave it to us, and there was a name: *secondary infertility*.

With *primary infertility*, or simply *infertility*, a couple is not having success conceiving a child. With *secondary infertility*, in layman's terms, it means it worked once, but we were having trouble getting pregnant the second time. There was still a slim chance we could get pregnant, according to our doctor, but he did not give us much hope—or false hope.

He told us to stay on the medication and see what happens.

We left the doctor's office, completely numb at first. Then came tears and some discouragement. We were hopeful to some degree, but the bottom-line emotion was definitely sadness.

In the meantime, you name the emotion, and I promise you, we felt it.

Name It, Claim It

I was raised Jewish and came to faith as a Jesus follower late in my senior year of high school. My family struggled with my "conversion" initially, thinking I was being a traitor to my upbringing. However, even though I had been raised in the synagogue for years, it was never real to me. I attended Hebrew school but never felt true ownership of reformed Judaism.

My newfound faith was cemented my first two years of college, and I began to see that being a Christian actually was a *completion* of my Jewish heritage. Now as a young "Messianic-Jew," I felt connected to the Old and New Testaments. The Bible started to made sense, not as separate books but one organized book. I liked referring to myself as a "Hebrew Christian" or a "Jewish Christian." I felt fulfilled, and even though many Jewish rabbis told me I could not be both Jewish and Christian, I felt very Jewish. And Christian. I followed my Messiah Jesus, who was Jewish, too, by the way. I had become new. I was beginning to connect the dots with my Jewish roots and Christianity.

I was taught in my college years what is known today as the "prosperity gospel." Back then, we referred to this teaching as *"name it, claim it, and frame it."* If we wanted God to heal someone, we "named it." If we needed a car for college, we "claimed it." If the prayer was answered, "we framed it." The "gospel" asserts if you *speak* something into existence, it will happen. If you speak positive things like "I will be healed," you will receive your health back, and if you declare bad things like "My neck is killing me," then you will probably die of neck problems. This "health and wealth" theology can be dangerous, but as a college student, that was all I knew.

We practiced this "gospel" all the time. We told storms to "leave in the name of Jesus" and told tornadoes to go in another direction. We saw healings of cancer and miracles of money showing up in our college mailboxes. It was all so simple in those college years.

Fast-forward, as a "mature" man of thirty-one years old no longer a college student, I would put in my request for another baby, or order to God, and within a certain time frame, the Almighty would oblige, right? For many years, it seemed to work well, so I ran with it. Certainly, God could snap His divine fingers and give us another baby, right? I mean, is that too much to ask the Lord of the universe?

Everyone I met was asked to pray for another baby Olshine. Meanwhile, we also loved the moments we had with our little girl. We adored Rachel. She was a joy to have in our family, and we did not want to neglect her with our worries about having another child. We were crazy about our "Ray-Ray" girl.

Getting Desperate

None of the "miracle" medications were working to help us conceive another baby. The years moved slowly. I hit a desperation point. I began a fast, abstaining from food for many days as I spent more time pleading God for child number two. Rhonda and I tried to remain in faith, but at times, I felt God was nowhere to be found. I felt neglected by God.

I figured God had better things to work on, other "fish to fry"—as they say in the South.

I was taught as a young Jesus follower that God answers prayer in one of three ways: Yes, no, or wait. We interpreted this baby request as "no" for a long time, so we would keep praying. It was a cycle of fervent intercession, and then, for a period of time, I refused to pray for another baby.

I started to shut down emotionally and spiritually. I remember one week not praying to God at all about anything—not out of fear of receiving a "no" or "yes" or even "wait." I was scared of praying and receiving *no* answer. I was fearful of *God's silence.*

Silence seems *appropriate* when I am having lunch with a friend and we are not interrupting each other.

Silence seems *purposeful* when I am engaged in a good conversation with my wife and we are listening intently, with all the meaningful body language of our heads nodding in affirmation of being fully present.

But when God is silent, it feels different, almost alienating and isolating.

Time passed. Still no second child. We searched the Scriptures, and it was evident that "children are a blessing from the Lord." Maybe we needed to change the narrative and *start thanking* God for the next child rather than just keep asking, like a grocery checklist. We thanked God for the second imaginary baby for a few months and then quit.

News Flash

If you do not like silence from the heavens, could it be that you think God is playing "hide and seek?" As Christ followers, we *want* to hear the voice of God. Some are desperate to have a divine connection with God, yet it seems so *elusive*. Some of us were taught that God desires intimacy with his people. I *believe* that and have *experienced* some marvelous encounters with God.

Most people do *not* hear audible voices from God, like the apostle Paul did. We do not see burning bushes like Moses or have a visitation from God that makes us want to bow down on the ground, as did Joshua. Some will never hear a "still small voice" like the prophet Elijah, and some might never see angels like Jacob.

We have all experienced silence when it comes to experiencing God.

My friend, Craig, told me I was thinking about silence in such a pejorative way. He asked me, "Cannot silence be healthy? Could it be that silence is not bad or negative, that there might be *real purpose* behind silence?"

He's right.

What if silence *might* actually be an invitation to something deeper, more profound, something that pushes us to explore who we are as humans and the hidden mysteries of God and His heart?

With all this struggling to have another child, I began to think there was another approach to our madness. What if we changed the storyline, stopped having a pity party and begging God for another baby, and started *celebrating* and thanking God for the one child we already had?

Novel idea! Rhonda does not worry like I do, so she was much more at peace with the process than I was. I was bred in a family of worriers. My mom, dad, and grandparents could get Olympic gold medals in anxiety. There was a problem—I was *overthinking* everything.

One of the advantages of being silent and introspective is learning to ask yourself questions. I began asking some realistic "what, why, and when" questions to see what was really deep down inside me:

- What if we never get pregnant again? Can we live with that?
- Why was I obsessed with the phrase, "We have an only child?"
- When did having two or more kids become the optimal prize as a parent?

My heart was curious to ask questions, and here are the three biggest ones that still haunted me:

- Why am I so preoccupied with having another child when so many couples are infertile?
- Have we turned this idea of getting pregnant into an idol?
- Where is God in all this?

The question of where is God in our circumstances was a heartfelt cry from King David:

> "How long, O Lord? Will you forget me forever? How long will
> you hide your face from me?"
> —Psalm 13:1, ESV

I wanted to understand more about why God was seemingly absent because I could not wrap my tiny little brain around the concept. For some reason, I felt like a failure because we could not conceive again. We sought some good therapy and wisdom from counselors and friends, which was very helpful in our times of grieving and emotional pain.

My head hurt thinking about all the possibilities. What if we laid down this desire for another child, as Abraham offered his son, Isaac, to God?

What if we "let it go?" *So we did.* Seemed like the right thing to do.

Baby Stepping

For the next five years, we sought to be content and joyful as a family. Rhonda and I have always been committed to making our marriage our top priority, with children next. We began to relax as we took the pressure off ourselves to get pregnant. The grief was waning as we refocused on each other. Time to bring some fun back into the Olshine family!

One of our family goals has always been to be playful, laugh a lot, and enjoy each moment. Eric Liddell, the famous Scottish runner, known primarily for his role in the movie *Chariots of Fire*, said, "When I run, I feel His (God's) pleasure."

That is how I really felt about my family—pleasure. I have great joy when it comes to Rhonda and Rachel. Rachel has always been spunky and full of life, and we did not want to miss a moment of it! Rachel was so much fun to be around. Rhonda and I both coached her in her softball and basketball games; watched TV shows together; and visited our favorite restaurants, beaches, and mountains as a family of three.

In the back of our minds, Rhonda and I still thought about getting pregnant at times, but we just started to assume that one child was God's plan for us. We became *comfortable* with that, most of the time. On rare occasions, I battled some bitterness over not getting pregnant again. Overall, Rhonda and I chose to keep our attitudes and perspectives linked in with Philippians 4:6: "Do not be anxious about anything, but by prayer and petition, with thanksgiving, present your requests to God."

We prayed for a spirit of thankfulness. We prayed for a spirit of non-anxiousness. We prayed for an attitude of gratitude.

We prayed to experience "the peace of God which transcends all understanding" and that God would "guard" our "hearts and minds" in Christ Jesus" (see Philippians 4:7).

We desired, as Paul stated, to think on "whatever is true, whatever is right and pure," and we certainly wanted to learn the most important lesson: "to be content whatever the circumstances" (Phil. 4:11).

After pastoring in Ohio and Oklahoma, we moved to Columbia, South Carolina, where I would become the director and professor of youth ministry at Columbia International University. Rachel was ten years old that year. We gave full-throttle commitment to her while she was in elementary, middle, and high school.

Life was good.

I was in my first year of teaching in the university and was out speaking a number of weekends each year at youth venues. Rhonda was teaching middle school. We were in our sweet spot.

My family would travel with me to speaking engagements nine out of ten times, and we really loved visiting new places. By the time Rachel hit her junior year of high school, she had already been to more than thirty-five states and seven countries. We were a traveling family! Our prayer for peace and contentment seemed to be answered.

Ready for a Baby?

As we were in the thick of raising a teenage girl, my wife asked me one evening, when Rachel was about sixteen years old, if I still would like another child. I responded, "I'm not sure. We are getting a little bit older." We were both in our early forties.

Rhonda proceeded, "I had this inner impression asking me if I wanted another baby, and I said yes."

(Note: We have had many laughs since that time about why I was not involved in this conversation with her and God).

On December 31, the morning of New Year's Eve (Y2K), Rhonda was having severe stomach pains for a few days, and I urged her to go see her doctor. Three hours later, I was at the gym, walking on the treadmill. Rhonda came into the gym with a funny look on her face.

She signaled for me to hop off. I told her, "Just a minute."

She asked again, "Please come here; I need to tell you something."

Again, I requested just a moment, and then I jumped off the treadmill.

She pulled me close and whispered in my ear these words: "I am pregnant."

I was in a bit of shock. Stunned, to be honest. Floored. And giddy.

We hugged each other in the middle of the gym and headed home to process the good news from the deluge of emotions. Later that evening, we went to our couples' group for a New Year's Eve party. Following dinner, we had a sharing time. Up to that point, we still had not told our best friends the good news about our pregnancy.

As each person went around the room responding to the question, "What do you hope for in the upcoming year?" eventually it came to Rhonda's turn. She said something like, "Well, I guess I'll be learning how to care for a new member of the family."

Everyone looked at my wife with curiosity. Loretta probed, "What do you mean?"

Rhonda said, "We are going to have another baby." The group erupted with laughter, applause, hugs, and kisses. It was a night to remember. Everyone celebrated with us, affirming that new life was on the way. We were all tickled.

Nine Months Go Fast

Rhonda and I had waited *a long time* for baby number two. Fifteen years! And now the countdown was on! Nine months to welcome our second child.

Our minds were filled with questions: *Will it be worth the wait? What if this is a hard pregnancy? What if this pregnancy fails?*

A few months into the pregnancy, one night we thought Rhonda was having a miscarriage. She and I were sobbing, crying out to God to save a baby we had prayed and desperately anticipated for such a long time. I wondered if God was messing with us, challenging our faith. A visit to the doctor soon after that showed the baby was still doing well.

Months passed, and finally on August 9, our son arrived. We knew it was a boy, and we named him "Andrew," meaning "strong one." His middle name, David (after me), means "beloved." By 8:30 a.m., Andrew entered our world. He looked like every newborn, in need of love, warmth, and a good cleaning.

An Emerging Storm

I spent most of that day at the hospital and then headed home to shower, take a nap, and call friends and family. At around 6:00 p.m., my cell phone rang. It was Rhonda. I picked up, and I heard her crying. She could barely talk.

The nurses and doctors had kept Andrew away in the nursery area all day. Something was wrong.

"Honey, they said Andrew might have *Down syndrome*."

"Down what?" I did not know what she meant. Having the word *down* followed by the word *syndrome* did not sound good to me.

Rhonda said tearfully, "Down syndrome —'Downs' for short. It is a genetic disorder with developmental delays."

I told Rhonda that Rachel and I would drive back to the hospital immediately. Before I could jump in my car, I fell apart. I cried uncontrollably on my bed for at least ten minutes, maybe more. Rachel started to cry as well, and then she tried to comfort me with the words, "Daddy, it's going to be okay."

For fifteen long years, God seemed silent about us having another baby. Now we had a child with a disability. In the days following, I would come to get an enormous amount of information about Down syndrome.

There would be a blood test to determine if Andrew had Downs. We did not know the severity of his genetic code because there is a spectrum of low to high functioning with this disability. Would Andrew walk? Talk? Would he ever be able to read? How much would he be able to understand? Would he play sports?

We would not know for a while.

What is Down syndrome, anyway? It is a cognitive impairment with some possible physical limitations. Trisomy 21 is the official name. Down syndrome is named after the English doctor John Langdon Down, who was the first to categorize the features for the disability. Symptoms vary from person to person.

I noticed in the first few days of Andrew's life, he had a gap between his big toe and the rest of his toes, a cute little flattened nose, and almond-shaped eyes.

Our pediatrician told us Andrew would be a gift from God to us, and he encouraged us to learn from him and recognize this was new territory for us as a family. Dr. Tye Whitaker told us that kids with Down's have an extra chromosome. I asked him, "What does that mean?"

"Kids with Downs have an extra chromosome—most people have twenty, and kids with Down syndrome have twenty-one. I believe that extra chromosome is one of *love*. These kids know how to love people like nobody else I know," he said.

Chromosome of love, huh? That does not sound too bad, I thought.

So Many Questions

Rhonda and I really wanted to have a great attitude about this, but the surprise of this new territory was unnerving and overwhelming at first. Our minds were racing.

- Was God toying with us?
- Why this, why now?

- How can Rhonda and I empower Andrew to handle this fast-paced world?

Oxford professor and apologist C. S. Lewis wrote, "God whispers to us in our pleasures, speaks in our consciences, but *shouts in our pains*. It is his megaphone to rouse a deaf world."[1]

God was *not* silent. He was using his megaphone.

The pain of secondary infertility, the pain of waiting for another baby, the shock of having a child with special needs, was a lot to bear. However, God was about to open a whole new world for us.

Rhonda and I had no idea what our lives would look like, but we had a feeling it would eventually change us forever, and for the better.

But for the first week of Andrew's little life, we were not so sure.

Big Takeaway: When you face life's uncertainties and difficulties, don't be afraid to ask the hard questions like "Why this? Why now? What is God up to? Is God doing something new and refreshing?"

Questions for Reflection

1. Can you identify something you've wanted badly but had to wait a long time to receive? How did that make you feel?
2. How do you typically react to disappointments? Do you get mad, hurt, sad, disillusioned, or feel some other emotion? Why do you react this way?
3. What do you do when you are in a setting that requires you to listen well and be silent? How do you handle those scenarios?
4. Dr. Olshine says God's silence could "actually be an invitation to something deeper, more profound, something that welcomes us to explore who we are as humans and the hidden mysteries of God and His heart." What do you think about that concept of silence taking us into a deeper journey? What does that look like for you?

---

1. C. S. Lewis, *Problem of Pain* (San Francisco: Harper, 1940), 91.

CHAPTER TWO

IN THE SCHOOL OF HARD KNOCKS

"I've begun to realize that you can listen to silence and learn from it. It has a quality and dimension all of its own."
—Chaim Potok

Andrew's birth in August 2000 brought an explosion for us in the new millennium.

We were definitely on a learning curve for a "new normal." After bringing Andrew home from the hospital, I realized just how new, raw, and unfamiliar this territory was. I did not know many families in the special-needs world, and I was not prepared for the many experiences Rhonda and I were about to encounter.

The years of being unable to get pregnant a second time were emotionally hard on us, but the reality of this surprise baby having Down syndrome was unlike anything we had ever experienced. This felt more like a *punch to the gut.*

We were about to receive an education.

Isn't that what life is about—listening, learning, uncertainty, and discovery?

On day four following Andrew's birth, my university's provost encouraged me to take off two weeks to process what had just happened. I was very grateful. On that very same day, I had a meltdown. I cried like a baby. My daughter walked into the kitchen and asked, "Why are you crying?"

"They are going to be making fun of Andrew in elementary school and middle school. Kids are mean. He may even be called retard or dumb,"

I blurted out.

I was being a bit irrational!

Rachel sort of giggled and said, "Daddy, don't fast-forward his future. He's not even a week old!" Profound words from a junior in high school.

Rachel's words really helped me, and in the weeks, months, and years later, "Don't fast-forward his future" never left me. It slowly dawned on us that something amazing was happening in our family life.

Although not an audible voice from God, I had this vivid impression in my mind: "Love this kid, because he will love you. He will teach you *much more* than you will ever teach him."

Two weeks after Andrew's birth, we received the official diagnosis phone call from our pediatrician. He said, "Well, I'm sure this news will be hard to hear. Andrew does have Trisomy 21, Down syndrome."

I thanked him for calling. I hung up the phone, both sad and angry because I did not want to accept this reality.

I had actually prayed that God would "un-down" Andrew's Down syndrome when I first heard the diagnosis. My prayer was answered, but not the way I wanted. God was *not* being silent. He was telling us three very important messages:

1. God was telling us, "No." He was not changing Andrew's genetic makeup.
2. God was shouting to us "Yes!" Yes, to love Andrew with all our being.
3. God was saying, "Wait." Wait and watch life unfold for you, your family, extended family, and Andrew. "Wait and watch me use Andrew for good. You will love what you see."

Lessons from Holland

Andrew's first few weeks were rough because he was not gaining weight. We made numerous visits to our pediatrician, who became a dear friend and advocate. Dr. Tye, known for his pranks on some patients and a plethora of bow ties, walked with us during a rough stretch. Eventually, Andrew gained weight and began to grow.

Dr. Tye would say to me over the years, "Focus on Andrew's abilities, not his dis-abilities. Look for his *abilities. Then stand back and watch his progress.*" Those words were profound, practical, and prophetic.

Tye's fresh perspective and wisdom empowered us and gave us new excitement and focus as Andrew's life unfolded before us.

My wife has an attitude of positivity. Rhonda would say to people about Andrew's birth, "The gift we received…arrived in a *different* package than we expected."

It was true.

We read a story called *Welcome to Holland* in those first weeks of Andrew's birth that guided us in our new journey. Emily Perl Kingsley's writing helped Rhonda and me process our feelings of both happiness and grief. The short story is about a family with a surprising disability, so we connected with it very well:[1]

> When you're going to have a baby, it's like planning a fabulous vacation trip—to Italy. You buy a bunch of guidebooks and make your wonderful plans. The Coliseum. The Michelangelo David. The gondolas in Venice. You may learn some handy phrases in Italian. It is all very exciting.
>
> After months of eager anticipation, the day finally arrives. You pack your bags and off you go. Several hours later the plane lands. The stewardess comes in and says, "Welcome to Holland."
>
> "Holland?!" you say. "What do you mean Holland? I signed up for Italy. I'm supposed to be in Italy. All of my life I've dreamed of going to Italy." But there's been a change in the flight plan. They've landed in Holland and there you must stay.

Having a child with Down syndrome would challenge us to learn a new way of life—a new, slower pace—with the learning curve changing almost daily.

We had landed in Holland.

Lessons from a Brave Mom

Raising Andrew, we would never have a dull moment, and we would

---

1. Emily Perl Kingsley, "Welcome to Holland," National Down Syndrome Society, https://www.ndss.org/lifespan/a-parents-perspective/.

work through the daily growing pains on how to parent a special need's son.

As he grew, Rhonda would take Andrew to speech therapy, occupational, and physical therapy on a weekly basis. It was during those years we met parents and caregivers with incredible and insurmountable difficulty. Many of these folks had unbelievable faith, determination and resiliency.

One afternoon I took Andrew to see "Miss Mandy" and "Miss Tina," his speech and occupational therapists. They were fantastic helpers and pushed Andrew towards new areas of growth. It is very accurate to say that it takes a *community* to raise a child, but especially for special needs families.

I dropped Andrew off to Miss Mandy and headed through the medical park looking for a cup of coffee. As I left the building, I encountered a mom who was taking her teenage boy out of the car. I had not witnessed anything quite like this before at the offices. She lifted the boy up, who probably weighed a good 80 pounds, carried him to a wheelchair that she had pulled from the trunk, and struggled to get him in. As she maneuvered him into the wheelchair, I asked if she needed any help.

She thanked me and said, "No, we've *got this.*"

I asked, "Do you have a few minutes to tell me your story?"

For about fifteen minutes, this courageous mom explained how her child was born with a rare genetic disorder that afflicts one out of one million children. Her story was heartbreaking, yet her heart was steady and strong. She described her life as "blessed," and her attitude was upbeat.

I did not know anything about her life. All I knew was her perspective to these hardships.

"How do you handle it all?" I asked.

She thought for a moment and then said, "God's grace. I did not choose this suffering. It chose us."

Sitting in Silence

I walked away from that conversation thinking, "My life is easy compared to what I just witnessed."

This mom told me her son would never talk or walk. He would never be able to feed himself, clothe himself, or go to the bathroom without radical dependence on his parents and supporting cast. She would be on duty with her husband pretty much 24/7. Thankfully, the special-needs community in her state has developed a respite program that helps pay for child care, so she can have a few hours a week to take care of herself.

I asked her, "What do you do when you have a full day to be by yourself?" I figured she would say, "I run errands, go to the grocery, treat myself to a massage."

Nope.

She responded, "I sit for long periods of time on my porch and think in silence. Silence helps me reorient and keeps me grounded when otherwise I want to go into a funk."

"Sit…and think in silence."

I was blown away by her response because I was experiencing the *same* lessons about silence, but in a different context. This "long and winding road" of seeking out where to find God in the midst of hardships might take me a lifetime.

Was I ready for the challenge to meet God in the silence?

Does Silence Matter?

In our culture, we tend to keep moving, stay busy, and task away. The act of sitting and being silent is not new. It has been around from the beginning of time.

Personally, I hated times of silence as a kid. I would go to the public library and start talking. My mom, dad, or the librarian would look at me sternly, place a finger to their lips, and say, "Shush!"

When you were a kid, did your parents ever send you to your room for breaking some rule, and there you were, sitting in total stillness, and you could not read books or listen to music? My dad used to call it my "penalty box" for making poor choices.

A kid's worst nightmare, right? Just sit on your bed and be silent. Penalized for a misdeed and sent to your room to be…*silent.*

We often view silence as a *punishment.*

But sometimes in those moments of dreadful silence as a kid, your *best ideas and dreams emerged.* Often in those quiet and peaceful times, your brain and emotions helped you come up with not only an apology, but also a plan to never let the transgression happen again. Or the opposite plan: "How can I find ways to do something sneaky and dastardly and get away with it?"

Silence is a great teacher.

Recently, I asked some of my Gen Z students to give me a word or an emotion that comes to mind when they think of "being silent" or being in a room of "silence." Here are some of their responses: boring, exciting, illuminating, mysterious, refreshing, restless, reverent, troubling, weird.

As you can see, there are many reactions, both positive and negative to silence.

Silence can educate and inspire us to identify issues within our souls that we *would rarely pay* attention to when there's a lot of inner and outer chatter going on beneath the surface.

Noise or Quiet?

I think we would all agree there are times when silence is disconcerting.

Sometimes I want the external noise of the culture to drown out the noise deep down in my soul. I cannot imagine going to a restaurant, dentist, or doctor's office without some background music. It's calming, but let's face it, it's still noise. And when it's not around, we get fidgety.

We love noise sometimes. We hate silence. However, there are many moments when silence is meant to be *normative.* Who wants a lot of noise when you are trying to sleep? Or take an exam?

Take, for example, going to a movie. Do you want to sit next to a gabber mouth who keeps talking the whole time and cannot handle the suspense of silence? Your movie "neighbors" must have an ongoing commentary of what is happening in the plot.

So annoying.

Hard Knocks Happen

Andrew's birth would bring about *new changes* in our lives—for the good.

My friends have told me I am not the same guy since Andrew arrived—that I am more loving, more compassionate, less judgmental. Tough times can do that for us. I think Andrew is turning me into a better man, husband, father, and Jesus-follower.

Dealing with secondary infertility, then having the huge surprise of getting pregnant, and then the bigger bombshell of having a special-needs baby created doubts, stress, anxiety, fears, grief, and hurt. I began to see that these distractors and detractors *could actually help me go deeper* as I explored the mystery of silence. We will explore that in Part 2.

I believe when we get quiet enough, we notice that silence is more a blessing than a burden. *Silence benefits our connection with God and others.*

Hardships stir up lots of questions, so ask them. Why not ask the tough questions no one else is asking? Children ask them all the time, and then as we age, we adults often get too intellectually sophisticated, all the while becoming a bit disingenuous, we resist asking the deep questions of life. These burning issues often emerge when life gets tough.

Two years after Andrew's birth, my wife received the unexpected hard knock of thyroid cancer. It was a stressful time, walking and praying with Rhonda, dealing with Andrew, and getting ready to send our daughter off to college. Rhonda's surgeon removed the cancer and Rhonda's thyroid. The doctor said, "This is the best cancer to have because it tends *not* to go into other parts of the body."

And I was thinking, "Uh-huh…sure." For three days, we had to sequester Rhonda from the rest of us as she was given radioactive iodine. We could not get near her or we would be exposed.

It was extremely challenging, but Rhonda endured it like a champion, and our family survived this incredibly turbulent season of life. God actually gave all of us a great deal of peace during that season. Rhonda has been cancer-free ever since, and we are so grateful!

Life Goes On

In the school of hard knocks, we learn what's inside of us, what we are made of. Hard knocks reveal our true character. None of us is immune from this school! Over the next decade, I would experience the passing of my dad, stepdad, stepmom, aunts, and uncles. It was rough.

And what held our family together? Times of prayer, worship, and silence, which allowed us to gain some wisdom and insight. Rhonda and I would cry, talk to God, laugh, sing, and snuggle with each other. We would go out at night and watch the stars.

We surrounded ourselves with godly people and those who cared for us. Sometimes we reached out to our friends who are psychologists. We did whatever it took to keep life fairly normal so we could continue to "do and live life" to the fullest. We took walks, road bikes, went to the lake, hiked mountains, and swam in the ocean.

The times of real health came when we slowed down. We looked for times of rest, play, reading, quiet reflection, and leisure—or as my friend, Larry, calls it, "downtime." Time to decompress.

And we noticed something profound.

We began to see a recurring theme: as we discovered places and people that helped us *recover and restore our inner world*, we found new life.

And not surprisingly, busyness and lots of TV and media actually dried up our souls and left us feeling fried and empty. As much as I love watching college and professional football (and I do love it), eight hours of it on a Saturday and Sunday doesn't draw me deeper into the life of the Spirit. It actually makes me tired, flat, and emotionally burned out.

Tough Times Illuminate

So when life throws you a sucker punch, and you are bent over with your head between your knees, a *new reality* is forced on you. Somewhere in the mystery of why things happen, silence becomes a *refuge*.

In the midst of trials and tribulations, we tried to stay flexible, having an open attitude toward God and an unguarded heart. We sought to have a posture of being curious about what God was teaching us. It is in quietness and silence that we learn about life.

Silence was the means for looking and longing to feed my soul and keep life somewhat sustainable.

Silence becomes one of the significant ways to enter a relationship of love. Silence is a way to love God and walk into His world. It is a way to love ourselves and others because it causes us to lean toward God's love and presence,

Silence is a *mystery* that we will ponder and explore throughout this book.

The Merriam-Webster dictionary defines "mystery" in several ways:

- "A profound, inexplicable, or secretive quality or character"
- "Something which baffles or perplexes"
- "Applies to what cannot be fully understood by reason or less strictly to whatever resists or defies explanation."

I really like the second definition: mystery is that which "baffles or perplexes." Silence is a mystery, especially how and why and when it works and when it doesn't work. How about the mystery of why God seems to be silent—can you figure that one out?

Mystery Raises Questions

I was at a bookstore recently. I wonder if, in the future, any bookstores will remain. I noticed that the largest section of best sellers was the one that had *mystery* novels. Murder mysteries. Mystery movies turned into e-books.

Everybody loves mysteries, correct? Nope, not everyone.

Mysteries sometimes have incomplete endings that leave us hanging. Stories with many unknowns. Some people love them, others hate them. We generally hate movies that leave us hanging in the end. We want it all solved and resolved. We don't want the story line frozen. We want all the i's dotted and the t's crossed.

The Bible is full of unknowns. We read of heaven but cannot fully comprehend it. We read of angels but don't quite get them. We cannot understand how God never had a beginning. How does God create things? How can God be three in one? Mysteries galore.

In Luke's Gospel, chapter 15, Jesus tells a parable about a wealthy family. The firstborn is obedient and keeps his room clean and tidy, while the second-born runs away from home and spends all of his dad's money. Eventually, the rebel sees the light, comes to his senses after hitting rock bottom, and returns to a glorious celebration. The father runs and embraces the son. A feast is about to be served, and the "prodigal" son is in heaven on Earth. Meanwhile, the elder brother is so angry he refuses to celebrate the return of his younger brother. The father pleads for the firstborn to come to the dance:

> "But we had to celebrate and be glad, because this brother of yours
> was dead and is alive again; he was lost and is found."
> —Luke 15:32

The story ends there. Frozen in *mystery*.

Jesus does not tell us what happens next. He leaves us hanging on for more. Does the older son ever go to the party? Will he ever forgive the younger bro? We will never know. Jesus freeze-frames the parable.

Mystery does this to us all: it forces us to use our imagination. It creates within us questions and curiosity. Mystery is profound. And sometimes disturbing, troubling, and confusing.

Jesus spoke of the "secrets of the kingdom" and "though seeing, they do not see; though hearing, they do not hear or understand" (Matt. 13:11, 13). Maybe you've heard the phrase "God works in mysterious ways." I never really liked that concept, but I'm pretty sure there's truth to it, and the Bible seems to support the idea.

Mystery Is Biblical

The Bible does not tiptoe around mystery. *Mystery* is a recurring theme in the New Testament. Here are just a few examples:

- "That they may know the mystery of God, namely Christ" (Col. 2:2).
- Paul speaks of "how the mystery was made known to me by revelation" (Eph.) 3:3 and "the mystery of godliness" (1 Tim. 3:16).
- "The mystery that has been kept hidden for ages and generations, but is now disclosed to the Lord's people" (Col. 1:26).
- "The glorious riches of this mystery, which is Christ in you, the hope of glory" (Col. 1:27).
- Marriage and the church are seen as a mystery in Ephesians 5:28–32.
- The fact that the Gospel means 'good news" is considered a mystery (Eph. 6:19).
- Christ is even considered a mystery (Eph. 3:4).
- God's will is considered a mystery (Eph. 1:9–10).

There are many more verses about mystery in the Word of God. You get the point.

Silence Is Biblical

The Bible does not shy away from talking about silence and those times when God seems silent.

What is the essence of silence? What is its nature and purpose? Is it to hear His voice? Is silence primarily to sit and bask in the presence of God? Is it both, and is there more? Why do I hate silence yet need it?

There is a mystery to mystery. There is a mystery to silence.

Ecclesiastes 3:1 says, "There is a time for everything, and a season for every activity under the heavens: a time to be *born* and a time to die." (Back in 1965, The Byrds sang this Bible passage and turned it into a famous song called "Turn! Turn! Turn!")

Ever wondered what your epitaph will say? Have you pondered how long you will live? *How* and *when* you will die?

What do you want your life to *echo* when you leave this world? What kind of story do you want your kids and grandkids to hear about your life?

Andy Stanley writes, "What kind of story do *you* want to tell? What story do you want told *about* you? The good news is, you get to decide. But you decide one decision at a time because you write the story of your life…one decision at a time."[2]

King David challenges us to do that very thing—to evaluate our lives: "Teach us to realize the brevity of life, so that we may grow in wisdom" (Ps. 90:12, NLT).

Andrew's birth actually was a catalyst for me to begin reflecting how I wanted to live the rest of my life. It somehow put me in touch with my own mortality. *Reflection can bring wisdom.* Teach us to number our days, Lord. Thinking deeply about our lives is a template for all of us to consider. What really matters for you? What is on your priority list? And what better way to ponder and process life than through the life of hard knocks and the mystery of silence?

Hardships Often Produce Values

In the classic movie *A League of Their Own*, Dottie Hinson, played by Geena Davis, is the star catcher in a women's baseball league. Her husband has returned from the war, and she decides to quit right before

---

2. Andy Stanley, *Better Decisions, Fewer Regrets: 5 Questions to Help You Determine Your Next Move* (Grand Rapids. MI: Zondervan, 2020), 53.

the World Series. To the chagrin of her manager, Jimmy Dugan (Tom Hanks), he's not a happy camper. "Baseball is what gets inside of you," he says. "It's what lights you up. You can't deny that."

Dottie: "It just got too hard."

Jimmy: "It's supposed to be hard. If it weren't hard, everyone would do it. The hard is what makes it great."

If it weren't hard, everyone would do it. Life is tough, and following Jesus is hard, but what makes it great is that it's *not* easy. Loving God is not always easy—neither is loving people or listening to the whisper of the Spirt.

There are 613 commandments in the Old Testament. The Pharisees were a zealous religious group who continually challenged Jesus. They were a pain in the rear to everyone, especially to the One they rejected as Messiah.

They were kind of like PhDs in religion—legalists, great at judging others. You might have heard the phrase "Do not judge" and thought it was from various political TV antagonists, but it is a saying from Jesus (see Matthew 7:1). He also asked the Pharisees, "Why do you look at the speck in your brother's eye and pay no attention to the plank in your own eye?" (Matt. 7:3)

For the Pharisees, their way of thinking about God was "our way or the highway." They definitely knew their Bible—most of them could quote any text verbatim from Genesis to Malachi. Some had memorized the entire Old Testament.

One of their leaders asked Jesus which is the greatest of all the commandments. This was a trick question. Jesus quoted the Shema in Deuteronomy 6, the foundational passage for every Jewish person. "Love the Lord your God with all your heart and with all your soul and with all our mind. This is the great and first commandment."

Every person in the audience listening to Jesus knew the Shema, because it was prayed three times a day in every Jewish home. Then Jesus threw in Leviticus 19:18 as a surprise text---"the second is like it: You shall love your neighbor as yourself" (see Matthew 22:37–39, ESV).

Priorities one and two, tied together: *Love God, love people.* Pretty simple, huh? Easy to talk about, not so simple to implement. Jesus believed that loving God and loving others were the two main things.

Jesus says *all* the Law (Torah) and the prophets hang on *these two* commandments. He boils 613 commandments down to two values, summed up really in one word: *love*. This was a big deal to Jesus!

Learning to love God and others is often *forged* through the school of hard knocks.

Nobody likes pain and suffering; however, sometimes it takes crisis and difficulty to get people to *own* those values. It certainly has in my life.

Andrew's birth and life have taught me so much about love. Andrew loves us well. Would we learn to reciprocate?

The school of hard knocks helps us face ourselves and hopefully moves us toward Jesus and others. The reality is that the Scriptures promise difficulty, suffering, and death. The Bible does not tiptoe around or skim over such sensitive subjects; it promises many things to us who follow Jesus. Unfortunately, adversity is near the top of the list. Jesus says that in this world, "You will continue to experience difficulties" (see John 16:33, MSG). I hate it for everyone involved, but it's true that life is delicate. Some make it through the muck and mud. For others, the outcome is understandably troubling. Do we bend or break during the hardships?

Love and Silence

How do we begin the journey of loving God and people? How do we experience love as it relates to silence and the mystery of silence? Most of the time, I don't know. It's been a trial-and-error experience.

And while we are being honest with each other, don't noise and distractions keep us from the whisper of God? Love and silence go together. One cannot be a great friend and a poor listener.

I have identified three steps for embracing God's voice and loving people.

Step 1: Acknowledge that your mind is racing with thoughts and noises.
We have to be cognizant of the clamors and identify the internal and external reverberations that distract us. Think about when you are trying to go to sleep. Is your mind wired with thoughts and ideas? Are you amped up from social media? Is your brain going nonstop? What is going on inside of your soul?

Do you find yourself constantly reaching for your phone? Email?

ESPN? The news? Do you really need to see fifteen meaningless emails about health, your Twitter feed, and Instagram's newest picture?

Why are we drawn to listening to sports talk shows the moment we get in our cars? Why on Earth does the guy in the swimming pool need to have ear pods on to listen to music while he swims laps? Seriously. I go to the pool to get away from my phone, music, and all the noise from my local radio station.

Can you avoid the latest breaking news for five minutes or the ridiculous YouTube video of a teenager crashing his skateboard?

Jackson Browne wrote a classic song, "Running on Empty." I resonate with the title of this song on many levels. When I am constantly on the go, running from meetings to classes to coffee with friends to a speaking engagement, I put my soul at great risk for burnout. When the well runs dry, I have nothing left to give others, and it certainly makes me vulnerable.

When I am always on the go, the voice of God is pretty quiet.

Noise, according to C. S. Lewis in his satire, *The Screwtape Letters*, has the senior demon referring to the demonic kingdom as a "Kingdom of Noise." "We will make the whole universe a *noise in the end.*"[3]

Noise is a major hindrance and hurdle in hearing the whisper of God.

Andrew's birth somehow sent me on a new trajectory of *slowing down*, pushing me to pay more attention to listening and silence.

Step 2: Take time as you go to bed, or when you rise in the morning, to practice silence.

Are you better at slowing your mind down at bedtime or in the morning? When I wake up, there is not much there, to be honest! I don't bounce out of bed in the morning like some, so quite often I need a hot shower and a cup of joe in the morning to get my head and emotions running on all cylinders. Then I can settle into some quiet reflection.

When you are ready for some silence, consider a few ideas.

Let your brain go. Take a deep breath or two. Relax. I personally like to lie in my bed at night and just be still. I get quiet and reflect. To begin, find a comfortable place with little to no distractions. For a few moments,

---

3. C. S. Lewis, *The Screwtape Letters* (New York: HarperOne, reprint 2015), 43.

drink deeply lingering silence. Find some friendly space in your heart and mind to know God more intimately.

Step 3: Look to an unknown realm where God lives.

For years, I have heard preachers and teachers say, "Jesus will meet you where *you* are." I affirm that, but what if we flip the script—What if we meet God where *He* is? What if there is a realm that we cannot see or feel, where God exists and lives, called *silence*, and one of the ways to find God and meet Him is to enter that sphere?

In a strange way, *God speaks in silence.*

God is always speaking; sometimes He speaks in silence. Through silence. Within the realm of quietness.

The writer of Ecclesiastes says there is a "time to be silent" (Eccles. 3:7).

Now is that time. A time to sink into silence. You just might meet God there.

Big Takeaway: Noise is a roadblock to peace. Noise is an enemy to being present to God. And learning to embrace the mystery of silence is the beginning of a new journey of wholeness.

Questions for Reflection

1. How do you interpret life when you desire some outcome to be positive and it turns out negative?
2. What things do you typically do when it seems like God is being silent?
3. How do you feel about getting silent and putting some solitude in your life? Is it uncomfortable? Refreshing? Explain.
4. Do you generally like noise or silence? What do you think has made you feel this way about solitude?

CHAPTER THREE

SOUNDS OF SILENCE: WHY YOUR SOUL NEEDS THE SABBATH

"Never miss a good chance to shut up."
—Will Rogers

Imagine your boss calling you into his or her office with these words: "You cannot have one day off a week. I am going to give you a paid break of *six months*."

What?!? Six months...awesome!

All of a sudden, you feel semi-retired, with little to no real daily agenda. This is what a *sabbatical* is. Instead of one day of rest, you are given an extended period to rest, play, and get restored. Think of it this way: a sabbatical is a time to emotionally and mentally get away from what you call "work." Some take it with the intent of more rest and play. Some see it as a way to deepen their prayer life and study time. Maybe it's a season of exploring new habits and hobbies. It's a reprieve from your "normal" way of life.

According to the Merriam-Webster dictionary, we tend to think of a sabbatical in academic terms, as a school year free from teaching duties that can be devoted to research, travel, and writing. In many academic settings, professors are allowed to take a sabbatical every seventh year. But a sabbatical is related to Sabbath, which refers to the biblical day of rest, or the seventh day. Both sabbatical and Sabbath originate from the Greek word sabaton, which traces to the Hebrew word shabbāth, meaning "rest."[1]

---

1. "The History of Sabbatical and Sabbath: Take a Break," Merriam-Webster, https://www.merriam-webster.com/dictionary/Sabbath.

Both *sabbatical* and *Sabbath* stress the importance of taking a break.

When Andrew was about two years old, I was offered my first paid sabbatical. It could not have happened at a better time, and it is one of the many great perks my university offers to faculty. Not every professor takes one, but it is available every four years to full-time faculty who apply and receive permission to take the semester off, which lasts about six months, although some stretch it to eight months.

It is not a designated time to be lazy, although it does provide a different routine and cadence—and there is no grading of papers! Some of my sabbatical days were boring, to be honest, and then I realized I needed to *incorporate* boredom into my weekly Sabbath as a model.

Over a period of twenty-five years, I had a total of four sabbaticals. Each one was different:

Sabbatical 1

During my first sabbatical, I was clueless about what to do, and even though my dean gave me some advice, I was restless. I spoke at a ton of youth-group meetings, retreats, and conferences, and I took a few nice trips. The sabbatical time was enjoyable, and I felt like I was making an impact. I was spending a lot of time navigating those early years with Andrew and special needs. It gave me much precious time with my son. However, it was not restful. I felt busier than when I wasn't on sabbatical! I had no idea that a sabbatical is about doing less, not more. I did not know that the less I would do on a sabbatical, the more I would accomplish.

Sabbatical 2

I studied about adolescent boys and ended up writing a short book on the subject following my sabbatical. The pace was balanced, and I slowed down quite a bit.

Sabbatical 3

I planned and did several short weekends of prayer, silence, and meditation. This was getting more in line with some of the goals I had set for my sabbatical. I am a slow learner, so it took almost until my third sabbatical to figure out how to rest and "be still."

Sabbatical 4

My fourth and probably my last sabbatical taught me to relish sabbatical moments. Rhonda and I had our plan all mapped out. We were going to teach in the United Kingdom for a week and then tour Europe. Several months before we departed, I received an email from my dean that I had received the professor of the year award, called "Excellence in Teaching."

The university where I teach is among twenty active universities in a consortium, and each college offers this award annually to one professor.

My school picked me. I thought it was a *joke*. Really. I inquired of my dean, and he told me it was true. I was honored. I began to think out loud, *Well, I'll at least get a nice plaque*. It *was* a nice plaque…plus a great financial gift. I was blown away! It was the exact amount Rhonda and I needed to travel overseas.

On the first leg of our trip, we visited the Hatfield House, built in 1611. To our surprise, when we arrived; the hosts informed us that the house was closed for the day. We asked why, and the woman said, "We have a special visitor today."

"Prince Charles," she whispered.

So we made sure we stuck around, and lo and behold, the prince showed up with his entourage. We trolled him a bit until he noticed my son, Andrew, and me. He stopped and reached out his hand.

We shook hands, and then he asked me, "How are you?"

I told Prince Charles we are Americans visiting the UK (really, now?) and then heading on to Venice, Italy; then to Croatia; Athens, Greece, Ephesus, and Turkey following my teaching assignment in the Peak District northeast of London.

Then I got a bit nervous and said, "Well, the real reason I came to the United Kingdom was to *meet you!*"

He laughed and said in his great British accent, "Well, you have come to the right place."

Sabbath is coming to the "right place."

The purpose of my sabbaticals was, in essence, to eliminate the three things I love the most: time with students, teaching, and tasks related to ministry opportunities. I made the choice to stay away from campus. Now, looking back, that was a great decision. Choosing not to be on the speaking circuit at first was debilitating because it had become an addiction, so I needed to get free from that toxicity. Plus, I needed to see that busyness is not next to godliness! Dutch writer and Holocaust survivor Corrie Ten Boom had a great line: "If the devil cannot make you sin, he'll make you busy."

Some days, my *big* decision was answering questions like these: "Do I drink decaf or caffeine? Watch ESPN or go back to bed? Pray or read? Go to the gym or be lazy?" Even so, while on sabbatical, I gained a few insights on how to make the Sabbath more restful and redemptive.

Some days would be a play day, exercise, eat, and nap; other days primarily included reading, writing, and being silent.

What Is the Sabbath, Anyway?
I am so grateful my university provides this time to grow and reflect. I realize that most vocations do not offer sabbaticals, although I wish they all did.

Think of a sabbatical as the Sabbath on *steroids*.

Not everyone will be given a *sabbatical*. We all, however, receive a *Sabbath*.

God implemented the Sabbath for His people to take one day off after working six days. This is the starting point for all of us who want to learn about silence and experiencing God. I assume one of the reasons you grabbed this book is to implement more quiet time into your busy life. Chances are strong that you want to grow in learning *how* to Sabbath.

As you begin to build Sabbath into your life, be realistic and set some achievable goals because it does require discipline. Sabbath does not happen naturally.

Here are four key aspects of Sabbath:

1. Sabbath is creating a new purpose, perhaps a new existence.
2. Sabbath is a defined day to learn more about silence.
3. Sabbath is implementing times of intentional quietness.
4. Sabbath is a day to lean into listening and seeing God while you are quiet.

Sabbath Beginnings
The mystery of silence begins by figuring out what day will be *our*

Sabbath. That might be a different day, depending on your life stage and various job scenarios. If you come from a religious background, you might know most families from Judaism and the Seventh-day Adventist faith take Saturday as their "Shabbat," the Hebrew word for Sabbath. Practicing Protestants and Catholics typically observe Sunday as their one-day Sabbath.

Will Sabbath be Saturday or Sunday for you? Or is your day off another day? (By the way, I am using Sabbath and "day off" interchangeably).

The apostle Paul told the Roman Christians, in reference to the Sabbath, that "one person considers one day more sacred than another, another considers every day alike. Each of them should be fully convinced in their *own* mind. Whoever regards one day as special does so to the Lord' (Rom. 14:5–6). He was emphasizing that each person must have his or her own *conviction* on which *day* to observe the Sabbath.

Sabbath (Shabbat) is a new pace and cadence.

I learned in my early years of doing Sabbath that if I am always going, always busy, constantly moving, I will never be able to really know what is going on deep down inside my soul.

I must stop. Cease.

I love this quote from the late, great author Dallas Willard: "Hurry is the great enemy of spiritual life in our day. You must ruthlessly eliminate hurry from your life."

Sabbath is a major step in eliminating hurry from our busy lives. And if we can tame the hurry-up madness lifestyle, we may actually hear the voice of God.

My friend, Keith Wasserman, is the director of an emergency homeless shelter called Good Works. Keith practices what he preaches: be generous, be compassionate, and love the poor. Keith always ends his newsletters or blog with "Love is a verb."

The dictionary presents "Sabbath" as a noun, but I encourage you to think of it as a *verb*. If you have never tried it before, get after it. You will begin to recover and renew your life. Learning to take the foot off the gas pedal for one day a week is liberating. At first, you might feel that you are wasting time and not being "productive." Remember that the goal of Sabbath is to get away from the mentality of having to produce! Ruthlessly eliminate hurry.

I have often thought of Sabbath like the concept of fasting. *Fasting* is the act of abstaining from food for spiritual or physical reasons. We hear of Moses and Jesus fasting for forty days. Fasting has become popular these days. You will listen to people say they are fasting from TV or social media or from chocolate or alcohol for Lent. When you fast, you are not giving up food forever, but just for several hours or days.

Think of Sabbath as *fasting from work*. It's not giving up work forever—just one day a week. By recognizing your Sabbath, you are not giving up work as a lifestyle. It's not retirement. Sabbath is intended to reduce the pressures and weight of your vocation off your shoulders, get some alone time, embrace silence and solitude, create some new buffers and boundaries, turn off the engine, and relish the downtime.

Our lives are too hectic. Our schedules are too fast paced. You and I need quiet.

Sabbath is meant to create some radical hush in our souls. Sabbath is fasting from noise and busyness. Sabbath will help take care of your soul.

Called to "Shabbat"

Why is Sabbath so vital, and what can we do about it as it relates to silence and residing in the presence of God?

In his excellent book *Subversive Sabbath*, A. J. Swoboda says this about Sabbath:

> Sabbath is the ancient idea and practice of intentional rest that has long been discarded by much of the church and our world. Sabbath is not new. Sabbath is just new to us. Historically, Christians have kept some form or another of the Sabbath for some two thousand years. It has largely been forgotten by the church, which has uncritically mimicked the rhythms of the industrial and success-obsessed West. It is not as though we do not love God—we love God deeply. We just do not know how to sit with God anymore.[2]

Swoboda continues:

---

2. A. J. Swoboda, *Subversive Sabbath: The Surprising Power of Rest in a Nonstop World* (Grand Rapids. MI: Baker Publishing Group, 2018), 5.

Because we pastors rarely practice Sabbath; we rarely preach Sabbath. And because we do not preach the Sabbath, our congregations are not challenged to take it seriously themselves. The result of our Sabbath amnesia is that we have become perhaps the most emotionally exhausted, psychologically overworked, spiritually, malnourished people in history.[3]

1. God calls us all to "Shabbat" because He modeled it.

Six days to work, one off. God has wired that system into the DNA of the universe, and to break it is to mess up God's original intent. We Sabbath because God took a Sabbath, plain and simple.

In my middle school years, I was the drummer in a band.

It was apparent that the one band member who could easily ruin the syncopated beat and unity was *me*, the drummer. The drummer has the power to throw the whole thing off.

Playing drums is like Sabbath—it has a particular cadence. Six days on, one day off. The Sabbath, just like drums, has a particular beat to it.

To not embrace, delight in, and celebrate Sabbath will mess *our* whole system and rhythm off as well. It will throw us off-kilter.

2. God rested; we are to rest.

I wish I could tell you that I have known the value of Sabbath all along, but I did not understand it growing up as a Jewish kid attending the synagogue. It wasn't even a high value when I became a Christ-follower in late high school and college.

My last week of seminary would change everything.

My roommate, Dan Hawk, and I were walking through a crowded area when one of our esteemed professors, Dr. Donald Joy, asked if he could have a minute with us. He pulled us aside in a classroom and said, "I have watched you two for three years. David and Dan, you both have so much energy and passion and electricity in your being that I'm scared that five years from now you will be out of the ministry because of burnout. So please promise me one thing—not for my sake, but for yours. Please start out your ministry with the right foundation. Etch out on your

---

3. Ibid., 72.

calendar a day of *no* ministry once a week. No church work, no speaking or mentoring. No work—period. Set in stone a day off, a Sabbath. It will help your six days be productive, and you will be empowered for the long haul. It may just save your life."

He was correct—Sabbath saved my life. *This is the essence of Sabbath: resting.*

Sabbath is not about legalism or rules. It's a time to establish a new rhythm. Thank you, God, for saving my ministry, my marriage, and my life. Thank you, Don Joy, for confronting me to set margins and institute a lifelong practice of Sabbath. Thank you, God, for the day of rest you call Sabbath.

Why do we need to rest? God commands us to *rest* because He rested: "By the seventh day God had completed His work which He had done, and He rested on the seventh day from all his work which He had done" (Gen. 2:2, NASB).

Why did God rest when He does not need it? God does not get tired like we humans do. Is there something beneath the surface of rest that we need to discover? Why did the Creator of all things, who does not "sleep nor slumber," create Sabbath?

I think the answer is simple: God is setting an *example* for us, a principle to guide us to a longer and healthier lifestyle, a template to guide us in living a life of balance. There are consequences and problems for those who choose to be Sabbath breakers.

Daryl, a friend of mine who used to run a large investment firm, has been hospitalized twenty-plus times for heart issues. His cardiologist told him, "Working seventy to eighty hours a week is slowly killing you."

"I had not taken a day off in over twenty years," he told me.

We cannot afford *not* to Sabbath. If you do not keep the Sabbath, the Sabbath will not keep you. If you and I break the Sabbath, it will break us.

It might seem counterintuitive, that we could be more productive while taking an entire day off work. If I work only six days and take off one, then how will I get all my work done? The answer: *You won't*, and that is totally okay. We all have limits. No one gets everything done all the time. Sabbath is really like starting a new routine or tradition.

For at least the past ten years, our family has followed a tradition of choosing one night (usually Friday) to go eat at Chick-fil-A and then head home and watch a family movie. I knew I was drawn to Chick-fil-A for more than their great chicken sandwiches and fries (and don't forget the milkshakes).

I was struck by the fact that every Chick-fil-A restaurant is open *only* six days a week. Closed on Sundays. Maybe that is what drove S. Truett Cathy's vision when he started the restaurant—to protect himself and his employees from fatigue by providing a day of rest.

The restaurant's mission statement is simple: "To glorify God by being a faithful steward of all that is entrusted to us and to have a positive influence on all who come into contact with Chick-Fil-A."[4]

On the company's website is an explanation about "Why we're closed on Sundays":

> Our founder, Truett Cathy, made the decision to close on Sundays in 1946 when he opened his first restaurant in Hapeville, Georgia. Having worked seven days a week in restaurants open 24 hours, Truett saw the importance of closing on Sundays so that he and his employees could set aside one day to rest and worship if they choose—a practice we uphold today.[5]

In that explanation, one simple phrase explains Chick-fil-A's philosophy, mission, and core values: "so that he and his employees could set aside one day to *rest and worship if they choose.*" (emphasis mine)

I think having Sunday off has enhanced the success and growth of Chick-fil-A and other organizations that choose to take one day off from work.

Rest Leads to Higher Productivity

The principle that God has hardwired into humans is this: by giving yourself one day a week to rest and recharge, you will actually be more efficient, productive, and effective than if you work seven days a week.

There is a great story of a wagon train of Christians traveling from St. Louis to Oregon:[6]

---

4. "Our Purpose," Chick-fil-A, https://www.chick-fil-a.com/careers/culture.
5. "Why We're Closed on Sundays," Chick-fil-A, https://www.chick-fil-a.com/about/who-we-are.
6. Marva Dawn, *Keeping the Sabbath Wholly: Ceasing, Resting, Embracing, Feasting* (Grand Rapids, MI, Eerdmans, 1989), 6–66.

They observed the habit of stopping for the Sabbath during the autumn but as winter approached the group began to panic in fear they would not reach their destination before the snows began. A number of members of the group proposed they quit the practice of stopping for the Sabbath and travel seven days a week. This caused an argument in the community until it was finally decided to divide the wagon train into two groups. One group would observe the Sabbath day as before and not travel. The other would press on.

Which group arrived in Oregon first? Of course, the ones who kept the Sabbath. Both the people and their horses were so rested by their Sabbath observance they could travel much more efficiently the other six days.

Sabbath renews, restores, and refreshes.

The Hebrew language seems to suggest that God started a new tempo and rest after creating the world. Woven into the fabric of our being, Sabbath takes us into a movement of restfulness. If God needed to cease, what makes us think we can keep up with the frenetic pace that drives many of us to workaholism and exhaustion?

I tell my university students that sometimes the most spiritual thing they can do on Sabbath is take a nap. (They like this line).

Take naps. Sleep in. Worship.

Humans were designed to rest. We rest because God rested.

A. J. Swoboda stresses just how important Sabbath is:

> So central to God is the ethical imperative to rest that it is established in Scripture before commands against murder, adultery, divorce, lying, incest, rape, jealousy, and child sacrifice. In fact, of the Ten Commandments, Sabbath is the only command originally expressed directly to Adam and Eve…The biblical story tells us that to rest one day a week is to be truly human, and to not rest is to be inhuman.

3. God established Sabbath as boundaries for humans to slow down.

In Exodus 20:1–17, God sets forth the ten commandments:

> "Remember the Sabbath day, to keep it holy. Six days you shall
> labor and do all your work, but the seventh day is a Sabbath of the
> Lord your God; on it you shall not do any work…For in six days
> the LORD made the heavens and earth, the sea and everything
> that is in them, and He rested on the seventh day; for that reason
> the LORD blessed the Sabbath day and made it holy."
> —Exodus 20:8–11, NASB

We seem to pay more attention to the others more than number four. We take seriously—at least most people do—numbers five through ten: "Honor your parents, do not murder, do not commit adultery, do not steal, do not give false witness, and you shall not covet."

Now, the ten commandments are outlined in more detail in Deuteronomy 5:6–21. In that passage of Scripture, the commandment to observe the Sabbath has the *longest* explanation of all the ten commandments:

> "Observe the Sabbath day by keeping it holy, as the LORD your
> God has commanded you. Six days you shall labor and do all your
> work, but the seventh day is a Sabbath to the LORD your God,
> on which you must not do any work—neither you, nor your son
> or daughter, nor your manservant or maidservant, nor your ox
> or donkey or any of your livestock, nor the foreigner within your
> gates, so that your manservant and maidservant may rest as you
> do. Remember that you were a slave in the land of Egypt, and that
> the LORD your God brought you out of there with a mighty hand
> and an outstretched arm. That is why the LORD your God has
> commanded you to keep the Sabbath day."
> —Deuteronomy 5:12–15

That's interesting, isn't it?

Sabbath is more than just a forgotten commandment. It is a *neglected* and *ignored* commandment. People do not realize that of the ten commandments, number four has the *most detail*. Numbers one, two, and three ("No other gods, no idols, and do not misuse the Lord's name in vain") are all short one- or two-liners.

The long, detailed description of Sabbath says to me that God wants us to get Sabbath *right*. God does the most explaining on number four than any other because He is serious about our health, our well-being, and our longevity. God is concerned about the whole person—spirit, soul, and body.

Sabbath takes care of the whole person, and taking a Sabbath is not being selfish. It is being a good steward of your life.

This command mandates that in six days, we should get all our work done, and on the seventh day, we are not to do *any* work. (Doesn't that indict most people in our world?) The goal is not to shame you if you are not pulling this off; rather, the goal is to decide *today* to start Sabbath personally and practically.

Now, pay attention to the Sabbath ordinances:

- "In it you shall not do any work."
- God "blessed the seventh day."
- God made the Sabbath "holy."

The Sabbath principle is meant to protect us from ourselves—from busyness; stress; the "tyranny of the urgent"; a lack of quality time with family, friends, and most of all, God. The Sabbath teaches us that we are humans, with the need for guardrails, and the Sabbath sets the tone for clear boundaries.

Sabbath is about establishing a new, slower stride.

4. Sabbath teaches us about true freedom.

Deuteronomy 5:12–15 reminds us again of the importance of setting aside a day from work to worship. In this passage, however, something is mentioned that was not stated in Exodus 20:8–11. In Deuteronomy 5:15, we are to "remember that you were slaves and that the Lord your God brought you out of here…" The observance of the Sabbath day, according to the text, links Hebrew slavery and the concept of freedom with the Sabbath.

God is trying to teach us that the *avoidance* and *neglect* of the Sabbath will create bondage and slavery; adherence to the Sabbath will create *freedom.* Work is good, according to the Bible. Laziness is condemned. The Israelites were in bondage in Egypt for four hundred-plus years and never received a day off. Never.

Twenty-four/seven, the Israelites were in chains to the Egyptians—physically, emotionally, and spiritually. Can you imagine if your employer never gave you a day off, no any vacation time, and no breaks at Christmas, Easter, or Fourth of July? It would be miserable, would it not?

I meet some people who work seven days a week and rarely take a break. The end result is that most of them have lost their enjoyment of life and have misplaced priorities. Some have even missed out on time with their families. Tragically, some have lost their spouses and kids because they have no clear margins between work and their personal lives.

Work is good. Being a workaholic is bondage.

"The Sabbath was made for man, not man for the Sabbath," Jesus said in Mark 2:27. Many of us need to hear these powerful words. The Sabbath is made for you. And me. Jesus is the Lord of the harvest. Jesus is the Lord of the Sabbath. Sabbath is about freedom. It is a time of renewal and refreshment. A way to recharge the batteries.

Working 24/7 is not the way to freedom. The best way to live is 24/6—God's way.

5. *The Sabbath is for intimacy with God through silence and worship.*
Hebrews 4:8–10 says there is a "rest for God's people." This "rest" mentioned in Hebrews is not primarily about naps or sleeping in; rather, it is about going deeper with Jesus, communing with Him. We are sometimes afraid of getting close to God, either because we are fearful He will not speak or fearful that He *might* speak! Sabbath is a time to get quiet, to become more silent than we ever have before, and to embrace solitude with God. It is a time to commune with God, to reflect on His goodness, to think about the riches of His love and grace.

In most traditional Jewish families, Sabbath is typically observed from Friday sundown to Saturday sundown. Whenever your Sabbath is, remember, the intent is to enjoy it, not to despise it. All of us need a one-day Sabbath.

Sabbath is about listening to the whisper of God. Developing a keen ear for His voice. I used to think of Sabbath as an entire day locked in a *dungeon* in silence. Nope—now I think of Sabbath as *pockets of silence* throughout the day. Sabbath is a time to take advantage of being silent. Not all day. Just a few minutes throughout the day.

Peter Scazzero says Sabbath begins with stopping:

> Sabbath is first and foremost a day of "stopping." We need to complete our projects…answer our emails, return all phone messages…finish cleaning the house. There's always one more goal to be reached before stopping. On Sabbath I embrace my limits. God is God. He is indispensable. I am his creature. The world continues working fine when I stop.[7]

Sabbath is a way to turn off the volume of both internal and external noises we battle every day. Noise drowns out our inner voice, which cannot find itself without silence and reflection. Sabbath is a way to listen to God. We cannot get closer to God with too much noise. In fact, too much noise will numb our souls.

Too much noise will drown out the most important voice—*God's voice*. When we grow in silence, listen, and worship, God is at work. When we lay our heads on our pillows for a good night's sleep, God is keeping the universe running on all cylinders. And as we slow down enough, even at bedtime, we might just sense God's whisper in ways we may have missed as we went about our daily tasks and routines.

Getting Personal

One of the simplest ways to figure out the *how and when* of Sabbath is to ask one question: "What is my job that I am doing five or six days a week?"

Let's get practical. Are you a physician? Youth worker? Stay-at-home mom or dad? Engineer? College student? Retired? What exactly is your job? Then determine what "work" that involves. My job is teaching college and graduate students how to do youth and family ministry. My five to six days of work involve teaching classes, mentoring, writing and answering emails, leading weekend seminars, consulting churches,

---

7. Scazzero, *Emotionally Healthy Spirituality*, 166.

speaking, and writing.

This is what I *do*; this is my vocation.

Next question: "What should my one-day Sabbath look like?"

Answer: Whatever you find yourself "working" at five or six days a week, cease from that activity one day of the week!

For me, my Sabbath means that basically, one day a week, I go from being an extrovert with lots of activity to becoming an introvert and doing none of the stuff related to my job and profession.

So, what do I do on my Sabbath, you ask? Most of the time, nothing.

That doesn't sound very spiritual, does it? It is, actually. Remember that Sabbath is not about efficiency or productivity. Sabbath is spiritual. It's about doing *less*. It's turning the engine off for twenty-four hours. It just doesn't look sexy. I probably will go to my indoor gym and swim laps. Most of all, I spend some extra time in prayer, communing with God. I embrace the spiritual disciplines of worship, reading, and studying Scripture—not for the purpose of sermon preparation, but to feed my soul. During these times, I may journal, confess my sins, or fast from food or media. And almost always, I will take a nap.

A. J. Swoboda powerfully suggests a radical idea when he writes, "A Sabbath day is not merely stopping our work; it is also stopping our thinking and scheming about work."[8]

Anything that looks like or smells like "work" for me, I avoid on my Sabbath. Some weeks, my Sabbath day changes. For example, if I am out speaking Friday through Sunday and have worked three days at my university the same week; that leaves only one day for Sabbath, so on that week, it's Monday. If I preach three times at my church on Sunday, then during that week my Sabbath becomes Friday or Saturday. If my weekends include no speaking engagements, then I will usually make Sunday my Sabbath.

My point is this: be flexible with Sabbath when life gets disorienting. Sabbath is a day to implement some silence, a day to enjoy and commune with Jesus.

So, how's the Sabbath working out for you? Are you missing out on the fantastic blessings of the Sabbath? Say to yourself, "No more 24/7. Today

---

8. Swoboda, *Subversive Sabbath*, 19.

I commit to 24/6. From negotiable to non-negotiable."

Six days on, one day off. Begin this week. Embrace Sabbath. God set a model for you and me to follow. Your soul needs it. I need it. We all need Sabbath.

Tune in to the sound of silence.

Big Takeaway: Establishing a once-a-week Sabbath routine and rhythm is the starting line to embrace the mystery of silence. Cease striving. Learn to rest. Listen for the inner whisper of God.

Questions for Reflection

1. What is your view of Sabbath? Have you ever practiced it? What does it look like for you?
2. What practical steps do you need to take to fully embrace and implement a weekly Sabbath? Lay out a plan, or it will not happen in your life.
3. How do you feel about starting a weekly Sabbath and entering a time of stillness, slowness, and silence?
4. What are the obstacles that would keep you from living a life of weekly Shabbat? How can you remove those barriers to make Sabbath become a reality for you on a regular basis?

CHAPTER FOUR
CREATE SOME PODS

"The checks of the Spirit come in the most extraordinarily gentle ways, and if you are not sensitive enough to detect His voice, you will quench it...His checks always come as a still small voice, so small that no one but the saint notices them."
—Oswald Chambers

Helen Keller lost her sight and hearing at the age of nineteen months. She also lost the ability to speak. "The problems of deafness," Keller said, "are deeper and more complex. For it means the loss of the most stimulus—the sound of the voice that brings language, sets thoughts astir, and keeps us in the intellectual company of man."[1]

With all the hardships facing her, Helen Keller could have ultimately thrown in the towel (and wanted to at times), but she did not let her disabilities break her down. She had a supporting cast who would not let her quit.

Keller forged a new way to listen.

She learned to listen by placing her hands on the radio. "Her sense of touch became so finely tuned that she could hear the difference between horns and strings with her fingertips. She also learned to listen by feeling a person's lips, face and larynx, including the lips of the second-greatest influence in her life after Anne Sullivan: Alexander Graham Bell."[2]

Helen Keller adjusted to a world of silence.

What do you think of when you hear the word "silence"? What comes to your mind? I think of ears.

---

1. Diane Ackerman, Natural History of the Senses (New York: Vintage Books, 1990), 191.
2. Mark Batterson, *Whisper: How to Hear the Voice of God* (New York: Multnomah, 2017), 57; Ackerman, *Natural History of the Senses*, xviii.

Many of us have ears but don't listen well. My daughter used to say to my aging dad, "Don't you hear good?" He was hard of hearing, and we found ourselves repeating words to him on a regular basis.

"He who has ears to hear, let him hear."

Jesus mentions this line fourteen times in the Gospel of John and in the book of Revelation.

Ears, listening, and silence are all *interconnected.*

How do we embrace the life that God has for us when it comes to silence?

Have you noticed that silence sometimes works to our advantage as parents with our kids? Let's say I get upset with my children, and I eventually simmer down. Then I get really quiet. They can tell something is wrong with me.

My silence makes them question: "Is my dad still mad? Have I lost TV for the rest of my life? Is he upset with his football team or me?" To get *their* attention, I become subdued. Silent. It engages them, pulling them into my world. Silence does that; it draws us in.

Usually, my kids will come up and whisper in my ear, "I'm sorry, Daddy."

To really hear them, I have to lean in. If the whisper is too soft, I may ask them to repeat those glorious words: "I'm sorry."

I think the silence we feel from God, and our desire to hear His voice, works in a similar fashion. When God becomes silent, it actually pulls us in. To hear his quiet, still, small voice, it means we need to get closer to the Communicator.

In this chapter, we examine four ways of getting closer to God on a day to day basis. I call it PODS, an acronym that stands for pause, outdoors, detox, and solitude.

P = Pause

Many of us have lost our bearings. Henry David Thoreau said we lead lives of "quiet desperation." We are spiritually and emotionally dehydrated. Let's try to remedy this problem.

One of the ways to break this non-sustainable pattern is to take a break. The McDonald's corporation had a slogan for decades: "You deserve a break today."

The concept is an old as the Garden of Eden. What is the significance of a pause? It is a decision to intentionally take two or three times during the day to slow down. It is a way to connect with God and be at peace in the middle of the day.

John Eldredge's great book *Take Your Life Back* discusses the significance of the word "pause." He describes his experience: "In the late morning…I pause, get quiet, and settle down. I give myself permission to simply pause, a little breathing room to come back to God and myself. My breathing returns to normal. The one-minute pause. I simply take sixty seconds to be still and let everything go."[3]

Try taking a pause. Thank you, John Eldredge, and the early church leaders before him, for keeping this concept alive in front of us. The pause has improved my ability to listen.

Begin with the pause once a day, maybe when your day is becoming hectic or you start feeling really stressed out. Then increase it to twice a day. Start with some deep breathing exercises. Maybe before you leave your house, pause before your drive to work. Or when you are at the high peak of anxiety, stop. Pause.

Leave this page for a moment and practice it. This is soul care at its best. Take in a deep sigh, a long and slow breath, and then release it. Take seven- to ten-second breaths from the gut. Then exhale. Then pause. Pray a prayer. Read a short verse from the Bible. Breathe in and breathe out some stress. Blow out the anxiety.

I will say, "I give it to you, Lord." And I name a specific concern, such as "I give the meeting this afternoon to you, Lord."

Pause.

I do it normally when I am waking up. I lie in bed, get the crust out of my eyes, and then take a deep pause, asking God to lead me throughout the day. I take a deep breath or two, in and out, and then start the day. I tend to pause again around 11:00 a.m. and at about 3:00 p.m.

I pause before I teach my classes. Just thirty seconds. Deep breaths. Then another thirty seconds. It helps me reconnect with God. It slows me down.

---

3. John Eldredge, *Get Your Life Back: Everyday Practices for a World Gone Mad* (Nashville: Thomas Nelson, 2020), 5–6.

We can all stop for sixty seconds a few times a day and be silent, right?

O = Outdoors

When I was growing up, playing outside was instinctive for me. My favorite class was recess.

After school, I headed home to get a snack and then immediately went back outside to play. My family had a big front yard, so we had games going on almost every day of the week. I have always loved sports: tennis, basketball, football, soccer, and swimming. My family taught me the value of getting outdoors and that exercise and competition teaches you invaluable lessons like discipline, teamwork, and endurance.

I spent much of my days from the fifth to ninth grades going to summer camp in the northern woods of Wisconsin. It was awesome. We had overnighters, sleeping under the stars or in tents by a campfire. Fishing, boating, and s'mores at night were some of the highlights. Six weeks of camp, away from parents—what a wonderful life for a teenage guy, experiencing adventures outdoors with friends!

We enjoyed the highlights of Olympic-like days of competition, leading up to the greatest overnighter of all time. All campers were sent out in teams with two adult counselors. We were given the necessary tools of the trade—tents, cooking gear, ponchos, and bug repellent. Northern Wisconsin was known for summer mosquitoes and black bugs that could eat your flesh off! We were taken several miles away from camp in a truck, blindfolded, and then dropped off in the middle of nowhere. This was too exciting for a middle-school kid! We took one main instrument necessary to get back to camp—a compass. Google and iPhones did not exist back then.

All teams had to spend the night in the woods with their counselors and eat dinner and breakfast. The first team to get back to camp safely won a prize. It was a blast. What a memory maker!

You might not be a wilderness expert or an adventure junkie, but spending time outside is essential to our well-being! Exploring nature is vital if you want to learn how to implement silence in your life. It is also one of the best ways to get closer to God. This is not rocket science, folks. I am certainly not the first to speak of the need to get outdoors.

We all need Vitamin D3 and must get as much time as possible in the sun. Each morning, I spend ten to fifteen minutes alone on my deck, soaking in the sun. That is my sacred time. It is incredibly healthy for the heart, nervous system, and well-being. I do not take anything with me—no books, no phone, no laptop. Just God and me. I sit and listen.

Most people spend way too much time inside. I recommend you do the following:

- Get outdoors daily. Take a walk. It's especially advantageous to go alone.
- Go to the lake, beach, or mountains. Just listen and take in the beauty of the world around you.
- Sit in silence.
- Find daily space between events and venues of your day to just "be." My friend, Mike, likes to say, "We were created as human beings, not human *doings*."

I find it fascinating that the Bible uses outdoor language. Adam and Eve heard the sound of God as He were walking in the garden. Moses headed out into the wilderness. Shepherd boy David fought bears and lions. David writes in Psalm 23 about being outdoors, lying "down in green pastures" and being led "besides still waters." This refreshed David's soul.

Most of the biblical characters thrived in the outdoors. Abraham and Esau were outdoor adventurers. Jesus and His disciples were constantly walking, fishing, boating, and hanging outdoors. We see Jesus often getting away from the crowds to a mountain to get some quiet time after performing a miracle. We read of Enoch walking with God for three hundred years.

The book of Ephesians uses the image of walking as a motif for our journey with God. Walking in the light. Walking in His ways. "Teach them to walk in his truth." Walking humbly with God to do justice and kindness. Walking describes our relationship with God. Walking with Jesus.

If you want to grow in silence, get *outside*.

If you want to hear the whisper, consider the great outdoors. There is something magical about walking or sitting in nature; it has the power to restore. If you want to hear the whisper of God, take a walk in the woods, where there is less noise. Without silence, God vanishes in the noise. If we don't discover some pulse of silence, we will get lost in the zone of distractions.

God gave us our five *senses* to experience Him: hearing, smell, sight, touch, and taste.

Go out and listen.

Birds chirping. Wind blowing. Leaves shuffling. Occasionally, the noise of a lawnmower and leaf blower disrupts it all!

The Word of God tells us to listen. Hear. Be silent.

God's voice is not just about listening with our ears; it's about *seeing* with *our hearts*. "Having the eyes of your hearts enlightened, that you may know what is the hope to which he has called you" (Eph. 1:18, ESV).

Silence also enables us to deal with what we recognize and perceive—our physical and spiritual eyesight through sharpened observation. Getting outdoors is eye opening to more than the physical world, but also the spiritual realm.

When I was thirty years old, I set a personal goal to visit all fifty states in the USA and thirty counties. I achieved the US goal when I reached age fifty-one, and I still have about seven countries to go. Why did I set this ambitious endeavor? One word: *beauty*.

The Grand Canyon is breathtaking. I kept taking pictures, and I couldn't capture the entire canyon in my slides. I began to see the same analogy of photographs with God. There is too much of God to get into one or two slides.

God is too big.

Even the most ardent atheist will tell you how awe-inspiring it is to see and experience the sights, sounds, and smells of national parks like Glacier, Zion, Yellowstone, and Grand Tetons. Ever ventured to Alaska?

You must try some of these extraordinary places. Acadia National Park, Maine. Haystack Rock, Oregon. Grand Prismatic Spring, Wyoming. Multnomah Falls, Oregon. Kauai, Hawaii.

The beauty in these places moves us without saying a word.

Lake Tahoe, California. Maroon Bells, Colorado. Angel Oak, South Carolina. Outer Banks, North Carolina. The Smokey Mountains. Spain,

Germany, Italy, Scotland, Ireland. New Zealand, and Australia.

Any majestic place on God's green Earth. (If I did not mention your favorites, please forgive me). If you don't have the dough to travel, just get outside in the neighborhood or local park.

It does something for the soul.

D = Detox

I like reading about how to keep my body healthy. All the cells and parts of the body are interconnected, and much of the literature deals with *detoxification.*

Detox. Detoxing the colon, lymphatic system, kidney, and liver is necessary to keep us healthy.

We also need to detox from media—you know, those smartphones that we own. They tend to control us rather than us controlling them. I am sure you know there is more information in that little square phone than the world has ever seen or known. It has some amazing qualities. The problem with this media magnet is that it takes incredible discipline and resistance to put it down and move it away. We need to detox from TV, the iPad, the iPhone, and social media on a regular basis because it is not only killing our bodies, it is also crushing our souls.

Spending time immersed in these devices prevents us from being fully present with God and others.

True confession: Sometimes I find myself not being fully present with people, leaping when my phone alerts me. When we do that, we send a message that the phone is more important than people.

So I started to make some incremental changes in my personal and family life. Would you consider joining the Olshine family in the detox revolution? Here are some of our guidelines:

- No phone use by anyone during breakfast, lunch, and dinner family meals. Ah, what joy and freedom!
- A one-hour break from the phone during the day for exercising.
- Turning phones off or to silent/do not disturb at 8:00 p.m.
- Once a day, going for a walk or sitting outside in silence for five to ten minutes without your phone.

There are occasions when students reach out to me for advice, or they cannot find an assignment. I tell them that if they contact me close to 8:00 p.m., I will not answer. It's not that I'm a mean professor; it's that I want to have guardrails for what is really important in life—time with God and my family.

Detoxing may sound too hard, but it really isn't as difficult as some people make it out to be, once you create the habit of unplugging from media.

S = Solitude

In a profound theological episode of *Phineas and Ferb* called the "Quietest Day Ever," Linda (Phineas's mom) is taking an online test and says to her kids, "I need it to be quiet around here…you might not remember quiet…I'm putting you on noise patrol."

Candace says, "She (mom) needs it to be absolutely quiet…I want you silent and invisible. Got it?"

Buford says, "Silent and invisible—what am I, a ninja?"

We would love to have some more silence, but as Phineas says, "Ninjas are renowned for their quiet and concealment."

How about some *noise patrol* or *ninja quiet*? If we are going to experience more of God's whisper and presence, we could stand some more solitude.

Peter Scazzero defines solitude as the "practice of being absent from people and things to attend to God. Silence is the practice of quieting every inner voice and outer voice to attend to God."[4]

Over the past decade, I have had a renaissance with admiring the writings of the desert fathers, and reading their observations about biblical characters who sought to embrace solitude. Learning to quiet the inner and outer voices takes time, effort and some patience. If we don't at least try, we will understand the Catholic writer and mystic Henry Nouwen words,

In his book *Making All Things New*, Henri Nouwen says, "Without solitude, it is almost impossible to live a spiritual life."[5]

---

4. Peter Scazzero, *Emotionally Healthy Spirituality: It's Impossible to Be Spiritually Mature, While Remaining Emotionally Immature* (Grand Rapids, Michigan: Zondervan, 2006), 148.
5. Henri Nouwen, *Making All Things New: An Invitation to the Spiritual Life* (New York: Harper and Row, 1981), 69.

He's right. In fact, once we begin the process of quieting our souls, we will see that, as Nouwen says in another book, "Solitude is the furnace of transformation. Without solitude, we remain victims of our society and continue to be entangled in the illusions of the false self. Jesus himself entered into this furnace."[6]

Bible verses like "Be still and know that I am God" have not come easy for my Type A-driven personality. These spiritual disciplines have been enticing ideas, but have not been a part of my strengths. I have read books on simplicity and prayer and thought solitude was a wonderful concept, but *not* for an overzealous man with a wife, kids, full time job and a full plate of activity!

I needed to act on my desires—even if it was a baby step. My soul had been suffocating on the inside for a few months. I was not panting or thirsting after God as described in King David's Psalms.

So I decided to take action. I did not want to do "it," but I intuitively knew deep down inside that "it" was the right decision.

What is the "it" I am referring to? I am speaking about going away for a three-day prayer and "silent" retreat. I was determined to get away. I had done these getaways before, but to be honest, most of them were boring and joyless. My wife was supportive. Time to try again.

I kissed my family good-bye and headed to the cabin.

Time for solitude and silence. I was nervous. Could I handle it or would one or two mediocre experiences turn me off forever? I was hopeful it could be life changing.

As I drove over an hour to my solitude retreat a quote from the movie, *Gravity*, came to my mind. Actress Sandra Bullock plays scientist Ryan Stone on her first space shuttle mission. Bullock is a single mom who tragically lost her young daughter.

While spacewalking, she says *"The silence. I could get used to it."*

I wondered if I would be able to get used to the silence on my time away?

I took my Bible, notebook, several pens, and a set of clothes for a few days. My hosts graciously allowed me to use their place and had even

---

6. Henri J. M. Nouwen, *The Way of the Heart: The Spirituality of the Desert Fathers and Mothers* (New York: HarperCollins, 2009), 25.

stocked the refrigerator and freezer with great food, so I was content with feeding my body. The challenge in front of me was meeting God and allowing Him to feed my soul.

Once I settled in, I was unsure of what to do.

Do I read? Nap? Explore? I headed down to the lake and sat on the dock in silence. The day was sunny, 80 degrees with no clouds in the sky. I sat for about an hour, watching the ripples of the water, birds and seagulls flying, trees slightly blowing in a slight wind—all movement, glorious slow movement.

I proceeded to lay down on the dock. It is amazing the power of our brains when we are relaxed. My only real agenda was to get still, and it was taking some time to slow down and relax. As I tried to enjoy the moment, the next thing I knew, I had dozed off. When I came to, I decided to take a walk. I headed into the woods somewhat groggy, and another quote from the movie *Gravity* came to my mind. Sandra Bullock was considering the fact that she would probably die in space when she said, "I mean, I'd pray for myself, but I've never prayed—nobody ever taught me how."

"Nobody ever taught me how." Even though I had been taught *how* to pray, I resonated with her words, "I don't know how to pray." There are times I do not know what to say or do, so I just sit in silence. Even if you are not a Christ-follower or religious, silence can be integrated as a major part of your life. Who's to say that prayer always has to have *words?* I walked in the woods in silence, communing with God, but I was quiet—no words, no requests, no pleading, none of that. Silence. I was simply seeking to learn about solitude, to get reflective, to reconnect with God because my soul had entered spiritual *hypoxia*—a condition that happens in our bodies when the blood doesn't carry enough oxygen to the tissues to meet our body's needs. I felt like that was my spiritual state at the time, and it needed to be corrected!

I spent days two and three much the same—reading, listening, worshipping, walking in the woods, taking naps, and avoiding social media. I started to feel free. I headed home late in the afternoon, processing my experience of solitude.

Lessons Learned

Reflecting on that valuable experience, I derived three important lessons that you might find valuable, too.

1. I had to be honest and admit that *solitude was uncomfortable.* There were moments when I felt like silence was not helpful. I mean, isn't part of the American dream about being efficient? I felt non-productive at times. My times on the dock, sitting and watching, were enjoyable, and I love my hikes through the woods. Nature has a way of restoring me. Staring at the walls of the cabin was somewhat monotonous, and the temptation to keep off media was certainly present.

2. If someone wants to get closer to God and hear his voice, sense His presence, *it takes determination.* It would have been easier to stay home. There was plenty to do with household chores and school projects. However, my soul needed restoration. If I was going to hear and see God, I had to make the attempt!

God speaks *within* us, within our hearts and souls. We hear God through our thoughts and impressions. That is where God's Spirit dwells, not in temples or church buildings made with human hands. We human beings are the temples of God. The Spirit lives within us, and it takes solitude and silence to be able to discern the voice and whisper of God. Sitting in the presence of God is not easy, but it is essential if you want the connection.

It takes intentionality.

3. Doing comes out of being. If I am always about doing (working hard all the time) and not being, eventually, the time will come that I have nothing to give or offer anyone. Being *precedes* doing.

"Slow down, Olshine," the inner voice said.

—

The Spanish artist, Pablo Picasso, was correct: "Without great solitude, no serious work is possible."

You don't have to be in crisis mode to begin with solitude. Solitude isn't for the weak at heart. Silence and solitude aren't just important when you hit a wall in life or are in the school of hard knocks. It's for any day—

good, bad, indifferent, or turbulent.

Mark Batterson says, "Silence is anything but passive listening. It's proactive listening."[7]

I didn't really want to go on the solitude retreat, but I needed it desperately. Henry Nouwen wrote, "Every time you listen with great attentiveness to the voice that calls you the 'beloved,' you will discover within yourself a desire to hear that voice longer and more deeply."[8]

Jesus knew the value, priority, and power of getting away from the hustle and bustle of people—not just to escape into nature, but to commune with His Father while alone and away from the noise of the crowds. Listen to Mark's Gospel: "Very early in the morning, while it was still dark, Jesus got up, left the house, and went off to a solitary place, where he prayed" (Mark 1:35).

Jesus learned to hear His Father's whisper while alone. The pattern and model has been set for us.

Noise vs. Time with God

How do we deal with all the internal and external noise and distractions? How do we begin to eliminate some of these voices that pull us away from the One who matters the most? I want to hear that voice. How about you?

I pastored a college church in a university town for almost seven years. It was a wonderful experience, and I loved hearing the stories of college students as they walked with God. Dave Smyth was dating a young woman named Shelley. One of the lessons I gained from them is that *time* is vital in a relationship.

I asked them what they meant by that, and Shelly and David explained that the greatest example of couples growing in love was learning how to spend time together. David said, "I cannot know Shelley if I don't take the time to be with her and listen to her." Shelley echoed the same sentiment.

Time = relationship. They know. Years later, I officiated their wedding. The Smyths have been married for more than thirty years and have three

---

7. Batterson, Whisper, 15.
8. Henri Nouwen, *Life of the Beloved: Spiritual Living in a Secular World* (New York: The Crossroad Publishing Company, 2002), 37.

young adult children.

The big phrase with college students back then was, "Are you having a *quiet time* with God?" It did not have the same meaning then as my book's concept. Decades ago, it basically meant "Have you taken *five minutes* to read your Bible and do a quick prayer and then get on with the rest of your day?"

Quiet Time

At the heart of this concept is not just how much time you are spending with Jesus. More than that, it is the amount of *quiet* time you spend with Him. Nobody talked about that part of the equation back then. Many times, God will speak to you in different ways than He communicates with others.

In college, I heard the voice of God in my spirit a lot when I was taking showers. I know it sounds strange, but it was true. I met God in the shower—not physically, but spiritually. The joke in our college Christian fellowship was, "Where is Olshine? Oh, he is taking a really long shower."

As I have aged, and hopefully matured in my faith, new themes have emerged, like being out in nature, or in a worship setting, or listening to music, or driving in the car with no music blaring. God reveals His heart in unique ways to us in different times and seasons.

Your walk with God is not like anyone else's. It is special and unique to you. That is why we say, "You have a *personal relationship* with God, uniquely yours."

Personal. Walk with God long enough, and you will get to know Him and His ways.

I still enjoy a lengthy shower to this day!

Practicing the Presence

Nicolas Herman was born in 1614 in eastern France. His family was extremely poor, which forced him to join the army. During his time in the Thirty Years War, Herman had an unusual experience. Staring and gazing at a tree with no leaves or fruit, somehow Nicolas intuitively sensed God's redeeming grace and love. He knew the tree eventually would spring forth with new life and that his life could be transformed the same as the tree's.

Nicolas Herman is known today as Brother Lawrence. Following his death, friends put together his letters and crafted the writings into a book. It is perhaps one of the most popular contemplative books of all time, *The Practice and Presence of God*.

Brother Lawrence's journey began by *gazing at trees*—doing the hard work of silence, prayer, and radical discipline of thanksgiving.

Listen to Jesus

In the Bible, the writer, Matthew, tells the mysterious story of the transfiguration. Jesus takes Peter, James, and John, his closest companions for three years, up the mountain. While there, Jesus changes before their eyes—His face shone bright like the sun, and his clothes became white as light.

They were alone—that is, until two great Old Testament characters showed up unannounced—Moses and Elijah. Moses represented the law of God, called the *Torah*, the first five books of our Bible. Elijah represented the prophets, who were spokespeople from God who relayed messages to the people of God.

Moses and Elijah were two bigwigs in the chronicles of Jewish history. Peter thought it would be a cool idea to honor all three—Jesus, Moses, and Elijah. "Let's make a little shelter for each of these men," Peter said. I have a feeling that Peter was in awe. "Three hall of famers right in front of me? Three awesome leaders of the faith! Equals."

Heaven had a different perspective. An audible voice spoke: "This is *my Son*, whom I love; with him I am well pleased. Listen to him" (Matt. 17:5).

The Father from heaven was saying that Moses and Elijah are great, but the message is clear: Jesus is God's best. Listen. To. Jesus. The law of Moses, Elijah, and the prophets all point to Jesus. Pastor Brian Zahnd says, "Jesus is what God has to say."

Moses and Elijah are great, but Jesus is the ultimate!

The disciples could not handle this intense and holy moment, so they did what traditional Jewish men and women did—they fell on their faces. In reverence for the Holy One. Jesus told them to get up, to not be afraid. And here is the moment we all need to pay attention to: "When they looked up, they saw no one except Jesus" (Matt. 17:8).

They saw only Jesus.

Maybe that is what Brother Lawrence dreamed of—*only seeing Jesus.*

Soul Care

Your soul wants to be cared for and nourished. Find ways to tune out distractions. Hindrances. Set your heart and mind to see only Jesus. Start with baby steps. It's a walk. Gaze at some trees.

Allow the Holy Spirit to whisper His voice to you. How? Start with the PODS. You will thank me later, and so will your soul.

Big Takeaway: Welcome to four principles of connecting to God: Take a pause. Get outdoors. Detox from media, and de-wire your brain and soul. Embrace solitude. You just might meet God in the PODS.

Questions for Reflection

1. How do you interpret life when you feel God is being silent?
2. What things do you typically do when it seems like God is being silent?
3. Which is your greatest need currently when it comes to applying the PODS acronym—*pause, outdoors, detox,* or *solitude*? Which of the letters do you need to implement right away? Why?
4. How do you feel about getting silent and putting some solitude in your life? Is it uncomfortable? Refreshing? Do you generally like noise or silence? What do you think has made you feel this way about solitude?

CHAPTER FIVE

DISCERNING GOD'S VOICE: JOURNEY INTO HOW GOD SPEAKS

"God is a communicative being."
—Jonathan Edwards

Following Andrew's birth, Rhonda's thyroid cancer surgery, and our firstborn leaving for college, I found myself needing to hear God's voice more. I was desperate for God's Word.

This chapter addresses the questions, "How does God speak, and does He speak at all today? Does God communicate to us? If yes, how? If no, then what's the problem?"

We cannot speak about God's voice without addressing theology. *Theology* is the study of God. Don't let the word *theology* scare you away. So, may I get theological with you for a moment? Thank you.

Theology means as we try to figure out the craziness of life, we must have some sort of measuring rod, some template to evaluate what is true and false. We need a plumb line.

Allow me to offer a quick primer on some of the ways God speaks to us, in the form of five truths.

1. God's written Word conveys His voice.
Most from the Judeo-Christian heritage would historically say God's voice and primary way of speaking to humans is through the *written Word of God, the Bible.*

The cornerstone passage that describes God's Word is found in 2 Timothy 3:16–17: "All scripture is breathed out by God and profitable for teaching, for reproof, for correction, and for training in righteousness, that the man of God may be complete, equipped in every good work" (ESB).

The apostle Paul tells his young disciple, Timothy, that Scripture has a divine power and purpose. *All* the Hebrew Scriptures are God-breathed, Paul says. They are inspired by God—they are God-breathed. The Bible is more than just a book or a manual for fixing problems. The Scriptures teach us about God. The Bible corrects, reproves, and trains us in being righteous. Scripture makes us complete, equipping us for every good work.

As my friend, Jeremy, says, "As we read the Bible, it reads us." The Bible, more importantly, is *from* God.

The Scripture is like a mirror that shows us who we are and who we can become. The word "Bible" comes from the Greek word meaning "books" or "scrolls." The Bible is often referred to as "the Word of God," a phrase used more than forty times in the Bible; the phrase "the Word of the Lord" is mentioned more than 250 times. The meaning of the "Word of God" or "Word of the Lord" is always a reference to God's voice to us, for us, and with us.

The Bible is an amazing book. More than forty authors contributed to the Scriptures. Their backgrounds are various: prophets, shepherds, kings, poets, fishermen, statesmen, peasants, scholars, intellectuals, rich, and poor.

Annually, the Bible is the number-one best-selling book.

Most people know about the stories of the people but don't really know the story of the Bible. The Old Testament points to the coming of a Messiah, and Christ-followers believe that is fulfilled in Jesus of Nazareth. The New Testament tells us of the Good News of God's plan for the world.

The Bible is the biography of God. Paul writes in 2 Timothy 3:16 that "all scripture" is used only one time in the entire Old and New Testaments. Most of the New Testament writings were composed before 2 Timothy, so it is doubtful that Paul considered "all Scripture" to include his own. He does not say "some" is inspired; rather, "all."

Pastor and Christian author Adam Hamilton writes, "All Scripture, for Paul, would have referred to those scrolls or documents that were considered authoritative by the Jewish and early Christian community… there was still debate in Paul's day as to which documents were authoritative."[1]

"All Scripture" being God-breathed or God-inspired is probably a reference back to Genesis 2, when God "breathed" life into his first humans. God forms Adam and Eve, breathes life into them, and they become alive. The apostle Paul would consider all the Old Testament writings, from Genesis through Malachi, as "all Scripture." The law and the prophets were divinely inspired by God, who gave breath to the Word of God.

Jesus believed that the law and prophets were "God-breathed." God's voice comes to us through God's Word.

The Bible *is inspired by God, but written by humans*. That is what makes it so fascinating. The writers themselves were *not* inspired, but the words God gave them were. We read of these narratives and stories and get a sense of the way God's people lived in their culture and tribal ways. Most Christians today believe the Bible reveals the will of God, but that does not mean every verse is to be practiced.

There are many commandments and prohibitions in Scripture: "Thou shalt not commit adultery." Thou shalt not covet." These ordinances reveal what God desires and warns against for His people. God breathed on the writers. The authors of the biblical text wrote the passages down. The words came alive.

God is speaking. Communicating to us through His written Word. The Bible is meant to do much more than give facts, trivia, or history. The Bible is not for head knowledge; rather, it is for getting to know the Creator of the universe.

The goal is not just for information, but *transformation*.

Jesus was raised Jewish, and as a rabbi, he read, studied, believed, and taught from the entire Old Testament. Jesus's most frequently quoted messages were from Deuteronomy, Psalms, and Isaiah. When tempted by Satan (Matthew 4), three times Jesus responds to the accusations by quoting from the book of Deuteronomy, chapter 6.

---

1. Adam Hamilton, *Making Sense of The Bible: Rediscovering the Power of Scripture Today* (New York: Harper Collins Publishers, 2014), 132.

Isn't it interesting to note that even Satan, the devil, knew and quoted Scripture to Jesus?

Peter, one of Jesus's original twelve disciples (followers), affirms the power of Scripture to speak to us: "Above all, you must understand that no prophecy of Scripture came about by the prophet's own interpretation of things. For prophecy never had its origin in the human will, but prophets, though human, spoke from God as they were carried along by the Holy Spirit" (2 Peter 1:20–21).

As we begin the process of learning how to read and understand the Bible, we must be careful to not take certain Bible passages out of context. There was a joke floating around for years that told about a young man who wanted to marry a girl and planned to honeymoon on some stunning island. He prayed and asked God to show him something, closed his eyes, and flipped opened his Bible. It opened on Isaiah 60:9 (ASV), "Surely the isles shall wait for me."

The young dude decided that God had spoken.

We need to read Bible verses in *context*, which means reading the verses before and after. The best way to interpret the Bible is with the *rest* of the Bible, not by reading isolated verses. Scripture with Scripture is the best way to interpret the Bible. In theology, we call it *hermeneutics*, which is a fancy term meaning to know and understand what the authors of the Bible meant when they put it down on paper.

I like how Adam Hamilton explains it:

> As we read Scripture, we are involved in hearing God speak through it. We may read a passage of Scripture and hear nothing at all. Then we read it again prayerfully, and we hear something we did not hear before. We sense God is speaking to us. Often it is as we dig deeper into a text, studying the written documents context, background, and the author's intention, that we begin to hear God speak through it. The Spirit also uses the exposition of the scripture in sermons and meaningful discussion in small groups studying the Bible to breathe upon us and upon scripture so we hear God speak through it...Through the words of the Bible, the Holy Spirit has

spoken and continues to speak. It is inspired, and it inspires.[2]

One of the best ways to discover the meaning and implications with some of the more complex verses in the Bible is to lean on Bible scholars, commentaries, church leaders, and the Body of Christ. Some TV preachers, popular podcast teachers, and mega-church speakers have not been trained in hermeneutics, so they just give their opinions. Be discerning when you hear someone teach. Don't be easily duped because someone uses the phrase "The Bible says..."

God communicates through His *written Word*. When you pick up your Bible (or phone app), pray and ask God to speak to you from His Word. Remember, the Bible is a relational book. God wants to have a relationship with us, so read it relationally and introspectively.

Study the text, and discover what the writer meant. The Bible must be interpreted—with the rest of Scripture. Look for the gems in Scripture to help you grow in knowing your Creator. Read a verse. Read it again. Then pray it out loud.

2. Jesus is the final authority.

God's written Word, the Bible, tells us that Jesus is the ultimate Word of God: "God, after He spoke long ago to the fathers in the *prophets* in many portions and many ways, in these last days has spoken to use in *His Son*, whom He appointed heir of all things, through whom also He *made* the world. And He is the radiance of His glory and the *exact representation* of His nature, and upholds *all things* by the word of His power" (Hebr. 1:1–3, NASB).

There is much to grasp here.

God's voice was first demonstrated through and by the law and the prophets. The final authority, however, is the Lord Jesus, who "has spoken" and is the exact representation of the Father. He upholds all things. The universe depends on Jesus.

If you want to know what God looks like, look at Jesus. Jesus perfectly represents God. Hebrews 1:3 says, "The Son perfectly mirrors God and is stamped with God's nature. He holds everything together by what he

---

2. Ibid.

says—*powerful words!"* (MSG).

Jesus is the final authority.

Higher than angels, greater than Moses and the prophets. God became a human being.

John 1:14 tells us, "The Word became flesh and blood, and moved into the neighborhood" (MSG).

His Hebrew name is Yeshua, meaning "God is my salvation." Jesus.

You might be thinking, *Well, I'm trying to hear the voice of God. Besides the Bible and the life of Jesus, some say that God communicates to us in other ways. If that's true, what are they?*

Great questions.

Perhaps you have thought, Jesus is not here on Earth anymore, He is in heaven. True fact!

The Bible says He ascended into heaven after the resurrection and sits at the right hand of the Father, praying for us. How are we to make day-to-day decisions about college, a new job, marriage, or a possible move? Are there any other ways God speaks today?

There is an influential thought from some Christ-followers that God speaks only through the Scriptures. I have a number of friends who fall into this "camp number one." They believe the Bible is the only means of communication today from God to man. They don't believe in modern-day miracles or the supernatural.

There is another perspective: camp number two. I have other colleagues, friends, and "brothers and sisters" who align themselves into camp number two, which believes God speaks primarily through the Bible but is not limited to only the Bible as God's voice. I am in camp two. We affirm the authority of God's Word. It is the unchanging, eternal Word of God.

Camp two believes that God can communicate in other shapes, forms, and ways besides holy Scripture. We in camp two believe that God can and does speak apart from the Bible, but we must be very careful not to believe every idea is the voice of God. Every impression and thought must be screened and confirmed through the written Word of God, with Jesus as the final word.

If it goes against either of these two main sources, I reject it as not being God's voice. Yes, I absolutely agree that God's voice is not only limited to the Bible. Even the Bible does not support that idea.

The Scriptures affirm that God speaks personally and prophetically, at times apart from the written Word of God. I am not sure why this bothers those in camp number one so much, but it strikes me with two more questions: Why do we try to limit how God speaks? Why do we insist on narrowing God's means of communicating with us?

3. The Lord speaks in various ways.

God still speaks to people. We can trace this from the Scriptures until today. One of the familiar phrases in the Scriptures is "God spoke to…" or "The Lord said to…" or "God said…." Most of the time, the authors of specific books of the Bible do *not* clarify in what manner God spoke to them.

We do not know *how or in what way* God spoke sometimes. Here is what we do know.

Moses heard an audible voice. God came to the prophet Elijah. Not in the wind, an earthquake, or a fire. God spoke in a still, small voice. Maybe it was in Elijah's head, perhaps an intuition or like a whisper in his ear.

The Word of the Lord came to even common men and women, and I am not just talking about the big dogs like Gideon, King David, Solomon, Zechariah, Peter, James, and John. God spoke to folks whom you may have not heard of, such as Elisha, Jabez, Josiah, and Ehud.

Why would God not speak to *us* like He did to these Bible folks? Aren't we just as human as they were? And let's not forget many great women heard the voice of God: Ruth; Deborah; Esther; Mary, the mom of Jesus; and others.

The Scriptures assert a number of other ways that God speaks apart from the person of Jesus and the written Scriptures. Here is a short list of how God can speak to us today:

- Angels
- Dreams
- Prophets
- Poets
- Music

- Nature
- Desires
- Worship
- Preachers
- Teachers
- Miracles
- Healings
- Promptings
- Thoughts
- Impressions
- People
- Prayer
- Open doors
- Closed doors
- Donkeys—yes Balaam's ass
- And more…

4. The Wesleyan view of Scripture helps us understand our faith.

God speaks to us in so many ways. I learned from my training at Asbury Seminary that the Wesleyan view of truth is viewed from a fourfold lens:

A. Scripture—the written Word of God
B. Reason—rational and clear thinking with reasonable interpretations
C. Experience—a follower of Jesus's personal experience
D. Tradition—Leaning into and listening to the history of the Christian faith and Church fathers

This idea originated from John Wesley, the founder of the Methodist movement in the late eighteenth century. Albert Outler, a twentieth-century Methodist theologian, coined the phrase "quadrilateral" in his collection in 1964 called *John Wesley*. How does one discern truth? How does one make decisions? How does one come to personal and theological conclusions? The concept of "quadrilateral" gives us a gem for identifying biblical truth, not to mention practical ways to hear God's voice.

John Wesley believed that God speaks through the *Bible*, illuminates our understanding by the *traditions* that go before us, completed by *personal experience*, and validated by *reason*. Wesley believed the quadrilateral helps us grasp truth and form our foundational views of life and theology.

The quadrilateral view helps us discern and come up with convictions on how to fully live out the Christian faith, with the Bible being the core and foundation for life, faith, and truth. The other three aspects—reason, tradition, and experience—establish a matrix for understanding and interpreting the Bible. Wesley affirmed that experience was vitally essential, secondary to the Bible, for determining biblical truth. These all work together in complete union and balance, none really working apart from one another.

These four legs of the Wesleyan quadrilateral became foundational for training men and women for roles of being clergy, of lay persons, and has become a primary theological guideline for seminary training in the Wesleyan-Methodist tradition. To any other faith traditions, whether Arminian or reformed, non-denominational or eclectic, the core principles of the Bible—reason, experience, and tradition—have stood the test of time.

This particular way of looking at Scripture is a profoundly valuable guide on how to think about the way God communicates.

5. The Holy Spirit is our "internal monitor" today.

God has given us an internal monitor—the Holy Spirit, the third person of the *Holy Trinity*—to guide us. Listen to what Jesus said as He was preparing to die, rise again, and ascend to heaven: "All this I have spoken while still with you. But the Advocate, the Holy Spirit, whom the Father will send in my name, will teach you all things and will remind you of everything I have said to you. Peace I leave with you; my peace I give you. I do not give to you as the world gives. Do not let your hearts be troubled and do not be afraid" (John 14:25–26, NASB).

Jesus is referring to how we will be able to hear the voice of God, and the answer is through the Holy Spirit. The Spirit is the indwelling presence of God the Father and Jesus, who will teach us all things and remind us of the things Jesus taught. The Spirit lives in our bodies and will give us peace in a way that the world around us cannot produce. Jesus tells us more about how to listen to the Spirit's whisper: "But when He, the Spirit of truth, comes, He will guide you into all the truth; for

He will not speak on his own initiative, but whatever He hears, He will speak; and He will disclose to you what is to come. He will glorify Me, for He will take of Mine and will disclose it to you" (John 16:13–14, NASB).

The Holy Spirit speaks the truth of God and comes to guide us into all truth. Whatever the Spirit hears from the resurrected Jesus, He will share that with us. My friend, Duffy Robbins, likes to say, "The process does not always look like progress." This implies it will take time for us to learn to discern the voice of God. It does not always look like progress. God's voice does not come to us quickly.

There is one radical way to understand today what God the Holy Spirit is saying to us on a regular basis. The key is that we must learn to *listen to the Spirit*. This is not a guilt trip or shame-game statement. It is the truth. Often, we are too busy and in a hurry to slow down long enough to listen for the whisper. I know this: God will not *compete* with our noise.

We don't look for angels, although they are around. We do not lean into expecting the audible voice of God because most people will never have this happen to them. We do not look around in our bedrooms for something weird and mystical to happen to us. We do not wait for a ticker-tape message from God in the sky or in our heads.

We get quiet. It is really the only way.

Listen. For the whisper. As the psalmist wrote, "Be still and know that I am God" (Ps. 46:10).

Ground Control: Back to the Bible

Getting alone with God and asking Him to speak through his written Word can be intimidating. It can also be thrilling! I mean, where does one start? Listen to these words from Matthew's Gospel: "Here's what I want you to do: Find a *quiet, secluded place* so you won't be tempted to role-play before God. Just be there as simply and honestly as you can manage. The focus will shift from you to God, and you will begin to sense his grace" (Matt. 6:6, MSG).

Find a *place*. Reading God's Word in front of the TV doesn't work for me. I'm too distracted. My house has two quiet places for me to go: my study and my deck outdoors. Find the best spot for you. It might mean an outdoor park or a coffee shop.

Have a *plan*. I personally like *The One Year Bible*, which steers you on a daily trek through the Bible. It is available in print and audio formats through many apps. My favorite app is called YouVersion. The blessing is that you have a plan; the burden is that there is a lot of reading. If a reading gets too long and laborious for me, I skip it and move forward. Sometimes, *less is more*.

The goal is not how much you read; it's actually more important how much you retain, and that happens in little bites. Not large chunks. Read short passages, and meditate on them. Take notes about what you just read. Read God's Word slowly, not quickly.

Pick a good *version*—one you enjoy and understand.

God wants to meet you in His Word. And if you get tired of reading, there are a number of apps that will take you through a daily reading of the Scriptures—just press "Play." You can choose the voice that sounds like he's from Wisconsin, for example; there are a number of British accents I really enjoy. You can choose from any number of versions. I love the NIV, but some like KJV, King James, NASB, or ESB versions. *The Message* is a modern translation that some people enjoy.

It's all about personal preference.

Advice for Rookies

For those new to the Bible, it is easy to lose interest or get bogged down in the early books like Leviticus, 1–2 Kings, and 1–2 Chronicles. While reading these books, you might lose interest, and you may even fall asleep. Some of the longer books by prophets like Isaiah and Jeremiah can be tough sledding. Keep plowing ahead, my friend. Don't give up.

The Bible's sixty-six books can be intimidating.

When I started dating Rhonda, I did not tell her everything about me in our first few dates. It would have scared her! I gave her a little bit of information at a time so we could naturally settle into the relationship. She did the same with me.

The Bible is meant to be viewed the same way. Take it a little at a time. Focus on quality. The priority should not be how much you can read in one setting; rather, focus on learning a little at a time and on what you can take away from it.

I suggest you crack open the book of Psalms or Proverbs and read verses on a regular or daily basis for practical wisdom and insight. The late, great evangelist Billy Graham read the books of Psalms and Proverbs every day as his devotional reading.

They were the primary books the mystics turned to when wanting to hear God speak. Meditate and memorize some verses. As you read, ask the Holy Spirit to impress on your soul what is most important for you to apply.

To get started understanding how God spoke to His people, here are five suggestions for books to read:

1. Genesis and Exodus (the first two books in the Bible) are great books to consider if you want a beginning place to learn *historically* how God was at work. If you want to feel better about your own dysfunctional family, Genesis will make you feel right at home.
2. I personally love Deuteronomy and Joshua for seeing God's message to and through some powerful people. Pay attention to the number of times these Scriptures say, "And God spoke to...," and to how those scenarios played out.
3. The books of 1 and 2 Samuel are inspirational, and you will see and hear the voice of God in extraordinary ways.
4. I read Ezra, Nehemiah, and Esther to discover how God speaks to us about leadership principles.

Four Categories of Bible Books

The Bible has what I call different categories, and if you can follow my flow, you will know what books to read and in what seasons to read them. I divide them into these four categories: fun reading, hardest to grasp, favorites for spiritual growth, and short and long and weird and wacky books. Let's look at each category.

1. Fun Reading

If you are new to the Bible, or it has lost its appeal, here are some fun books to read:

- Song of Songs is a classic love story, very sensual and romantic, about a connection between a man and a woman. It's a great book

to read if you are married.
- Ruth is a great quick read.
- I love the book of Jonah; it reveals the runaway rebel in all of us.
- You cannot go wrong with any of the four Gospels: Matthew, Mark, Luke, and John (not Paul, Ringo, John, and George). Pay great attention to the life and message of Jesus and how He spoke to people. I especially love Luke and John's writings. There is much humor in some of Jesus's sayings.
- If you want to see God's supernatural works of healings, audible voices, angelic visits, the book of Acts is your gold mine.

2. Hardest to Grasp

A number of books in the Bible can be hard to understand. You may need some help and guidance, but they are worth the effort. Here are a few in this category:

- Ecclesiastes is a great book for those who err to the side of intellectual questions, doubt, and uncertainty. It is a complicated book. If you have ever felt lost and somewhat cynical, this book is for you.
- Romans is one of toughest reads when it comes to understanding theology.
- Hebrews has some of the strangest concepts to understand, so to get a backdrop to Hebrews, please look at Leviticus, another challenging read. These two books are interwoven. Get a commentary to help.
- Galatians and Colossians are short books with a few verses that are challenging to understand.
- Some of the books like Job and Lamentations are somewhat challenging.
- The book of Judges contains some *Mission Impossible* type of action and murders.
- The minor and major prophets refer to the shorter and longer readings in the Old Testament. The minor prophets give a sense of God speaking through Hosea, Joel, Amos, Nahum, Habakkuk, Zephaniah, Haggai, Zechariah, Micah, and Malachi. Major

prophets are the longer, more prophetic books—Isaiah, Jeremiah, and Ezekiel. These can be hard to grasp without some Old Testament scholars and commentaries near your side.

3. Favorites for Spiritual Growth

These are my go-to-books when I need a shot in the arm on growing spiritually:

- The letters in the New Testament are also called epistles, mostly written by the apostle Paul. The books of Ephesians, 1–2 Timothy, and Titus are some of my favorite letters to read when I want to seek more spiritual growth on a daily basis.
- If I want to read inspirational writings, Philippians, 1–2 Thessalonians, and 1–3 John are my picks.
- The books of 1–2 Corinthians will help you understand how to live as a Christian in a decaying culture.
- James is the most practical book in the New Testament.
- The books of 1–2 Peter are relevant to hardships.
- Proverbs is hands-down the best book in the Bible on gaining wisdom.

4. Short and Long, Weird and Wacky Books

- Short books include Obadiah in the Old testament, plus Philemon and Jude in the New Testament. To me, these books are a little bizarre and confusing.
- When it comes to long books, Revelation fits the bill for being the most bizarre and weirdest book in the Bible. However, it is well worth the read on the "unveiling" of Jesus, especially the first three chapters, which are commonly referred to as the "letters to the churches" from the risen Jesus.
- I would add Ezekiel to the weird and wacky list. This book is basically about the destruction and exile of Judah and the promise of its eventual restoration by God.
- The book of Daniel is a narrative with some exciting and complicated prophesies to examine.

If you love stories with supernatural elements, sci-fi like reading, these books are for you.

So I read. Then I ask the Holy Spirit to help me understand and apply what I have read and learned. I ask the Holy Spirit, who inspired the holy writings of Scripture, to inspire me to grow and obey.

What Can We Learn?

Yes, God speaks through his written Word, through Jesus and the Holy Spirit, and a number of other ways.

Psalm 95:7–8 says, "Today if you hear his voice, do not harden your hearts." God wants to communicate with us. That is what makes this journey to hearing the voice of the Father, Son, or Holy Spirit so exciting and frustrating.

The famous passage in Revelation 3:20 speaks of Jesus's invitation to dine with Him. "Behold I stand at the door and knock. If *anyone hears my voice* and opens the door, I will come in and eat with him and he with me."

In the movie *The Two Popes*, Pope Benedict XVI is considering resigning from the papacy. He is in a state of angst and shares that, "When I was young, I heard the voice of God." That brought him great peace, but as he aged, he was no longer able to hear that voice. "Perhaps I need to listen more intently. I think, perhaps, I need a spiritual hearing aid," Pope Benedict says.

We all need a spiritual hearing aid, don't we?

Communication theory teaches that there is a relationship between the sender and receiver. There is give and take; there is dialogue. Communication comes from the heart of God. He speaks. We listen. Or at least we try to hear His voice.

The One who spoke the universe into existence, who spoke you and me into being, longs and desires to keep communicating with us.

Does the Supernatural Happen Today?

I firmly believe in God's supernatural power. There have been two times, to my knowledge, when God spoke to me in an audible, out-loud kind of way. I happened to be by *myself* both times.

I did not seek out any of these encounters; they came unexpectedly at a specific place and time. In each experience, I was surprised by the outcome. When the voice of God came to me in those scenarios, one catapulted me into immediate action. In the other situation, I said to God "No." Most of us know how that ends up going, right?

I don't believe that people who hear God's audible voice are any more "spiritual" than others. In fact, I think the opposite—that audible voices, angelic visits, and other supernatural experiences, most of the time as recorded in the Bible, seem to be directed at the most rebellious and hard-headed people.

Put Moses and the apostle Paul at the top of that list.

Moses was a murderer turned shepherd of stinky sheep who landed a job promotion of leading a few million smelly Israelites out of Egyptian slavery and then walking through the wilderness for forty years. And Saul the Pharisee, who contributed to the martyrdom of Stephen (see Acts 7–8), had a miraculous encounter with the resurrected Jesus and was renamed Paul, the apostle.

Both men needed some extra training and love from God to reorient themselves to the new way God wanted them to live. It took a burning bush and an audible voice to turn their lives around. They were both rugged and stubborn tough guys. Audible voices are not normative; they are typically unusual and should not be sought after, or you might get easily frustrated and disappointed.

If God chooses to give someone a supernaturally experience, remember, it is solely rooted in God's *initiative*, not ours. Just because we want to hear a supernatural voice does not mean it will ever happen.

God's voice is based on His *timing*, not ours. God chooses the environment, time, place, and moment.

We become disillusioned when we try to force God's hand to speak "now." I meet many people who will head to the mountains for a spiritual and physical fasting experience to "hear God's voice." If the goal is to manipulate and force God's hand, you'll probably come up empty-handed.

"How did it go?" I will ask.

"Nothing happened," most tell me.

What they really meant is that they came home without hearing an audible voice. That's okay because receiving God's out-loud voice is *not the goal.*

Still, Small Voice?

You will probably meet some Jesus followers who have spoken about a time when God spoke in a still, small voice. Basically, these are thoughts or ideas that were from God. I have experienced this a number of times as well. It is a mixture of intuition, impression, and a "sense" that God is speaking to us. A few people have told me the "still, small voice" was actually loud inside their heads, not so still or quiet. Other godly people I know have *never* had such an experience.

How do we know if these ideas are from God?

As I mentioned earlier, messages from God *will not contradict* the Bible.

God has spoken to many people in dreams, visions, through preachers, teachers, movies, the arts, sporting events, being out in the woods, friends, strangers, all kinds of people—and yes, our significant other. Almost all the time, people have said, "I know it was God because the idea was *smarter* than anything I could have ever thought of!"

A friend in college told me he saw angels—weekly. I have never seen one, to my knowledge. Maybe someday it will happen, but I don't seek them out. I have a feeling they are watching out for us.

Let's not get hooky-spooky here. Not every vision and dream is from God. It could be our own imagination or our flesh, or even the devil. So I always seek *affirmation* from the Holy Spirit and *confirmation* from godly people I respect and trust. God wants to speak to you and me.

Listen to God's Word

If you are willing to experience the presence of Jesus—to be silent, even for a few moments—then you will find yourself leaning into a new avenue of adventure. It does not take much courage to talk to God; however, it takes great boldness, endurance, and patience to be quiet and listen.

In church, we sometimes sing an old hymn with the words, "We are standing on holy ground."

Silence is holy ground. Take your Bible, and listen well. We know that God wants to get our attention. *Silence* can help us hear the whisper. We can all learn one major lesson: if we get away from the noise, we will have a much greater chance of hearing God speak.

Proverbs 17:28 (ESV) tells us, "Even a fool who keeps silent is considered wise; when he closes his lips, he is deemed wise."

The dominant prayer in the book of Revelation grabs my attention: "He, who has an ear, let him hear what the Spirit says to the churches" (Rev. 3:6, NASB).

Jesus invites us into a time of reflection.

This Scripture from the book of Matthew can comfort us during our times of stress: "Are you tired? Worn out? Burned out on religion? Come to me. Get away with me and you'll recover your life. I'll show you how to take a real rest. Walk with me and work with me—watch how I do it. Learn the unforced rhythms of grace. I won't lay anything heavy or ill-fitting on you. Keep company with me and you'll learn to live freely and lightly" (Matt. 11:28–30, MSG).

Crowd out the noise. Embrace the Word of God, for it is alive and active (see Hebrews 4:12). The Holy Spirit is within you.

Keep company with Jesus. "Learn the unforced rhythms of grace." You'll learn to "live freely and lightly."

I'll sign up for that one.

Big Takeaway: God speaks to us in many ways—through the written Word, the Scriptures; through the person of Jesus; through the Holy Spirit. God whispers through nature, teachers, thoughts, dreams, music, and silence.

Questions for Reflection

1. What has been your experience with the Bible when it comes to listening to God's voice?
2. What are some of the experiences you have had with God speaking to you in ways besides the Bible?
3. What do you think about people who say they have had dreams, visions, and other experiences of God?
4. What do you think when people say, "God spoke to me?"
5. What has been the number one-way God has spoken to you?

PART TWO

DETRACTORS AND DISTRACTORS

"He (God) is always whispering to us, only we do not always hear, because of the noise, hurry and distractions which life causes as it rushes on."
—Frederick W. Faber, 1814–63

There are many noises that distract us from hearing God's voice. Some are emotions, and some are obstacles to the faith. These voices come to all of us on a regular basis.

In Part 2, we discuss five categories of distraction that can rob us from hearing God's whisper:

- Stress
- Doubt
- Unanswered prayer
- Fear, worry, and anxiety
- Hurt and grief

Let's journey together as we learn to navigate these detractors and distractors.

CHAPTER SIX

GLOBAL PANDEMIC OF STRESS, MASKS, AND SOCIAL DISTANCING

"The word *listen* contains the same letters as the word *silent*."
—Alfred Brendel, classical pianist

The year 2020 was unlike any other.

It will be in the history books, and people will be talking about it for years to come. It's a year we want to forget, but we must remember it because there are many lessons to glean. My musings about our obsession for distractions and noise, our dislike of silence, our need for solitude, and God's seeming silence have been churning in my head for years. But in 2020, these thoughts lit up my heart in new and profound ways.

On March 5, 2020, I was speaking to more than seven hundred students at Clemson University's Fellowship of Christian Athletes (FCA). During the announcements that evening, Nathan, the host, asked us, "Please do not give out hugs or handshakes." Fist bumps or elbow bumps were permissible. Nathan explained that a pandemic was hitting America. My wife, son, and I headed home the next day.

March 11, 2020, was declared a global pandemic—it was the day the virus referred to as "Covid-19" or the "coronavirus" entered our lives. On March 13, President Donald Trump of the USA announced that Covid-19 was a national emergency and would eventually sweep through every nation, tribe, and continent. It was no respecter of persons.

I would describe the pandemic as one long season of emotional, physical, and spiritual upheaval, not to mention an election year marred by major racial tensions and economic disruptions.

Whether you are a person of faith or not, this virus created so many reactions: Fear. Doubts. Worries. Anxiety. Sickness. Unemployment. Deaths—lots of them. Globally, more than four million deaths.

When the virus from China hit America in March 2020, almost everything shut down. Walking outside your home felt like going into an invisible war zone. And, because there was so little trustworthy data known about the virus and how to protect ourselves from it, these things happened:

- K–12th-grade schools closed from early March through June. *All* schools went from residential to virtual learning. Students and teachers, businesses, churches, and synagogues communicated via laptop computers from a distance, virtually, through platforms like Zoom.
- There were no major sporting events for months, and college classrooms went fully online.
- There was no March Madness college basketball tournament at all (unheard of…*what?*).
- When professional sports restarted after several months of shutdown, they had only players, coaches, and staff in stadiums and arenas. No fans were allowed to watch. Eventually, in the spring and fall of 2020, some sporting events allowed some fans, whereas some states allowed only friends and families. It was bizarre to watch a professional football game with no fans, piped-in music, and fake sounds of people cheering or booing.
- Some graduations happened, and some went virtual. Most graduations for high school and college were canceled or delayed. For many parents and kids, this was a huge loss.

Our son, Andrew, graduated from high school in late May 2020. His graduation was orchestrated in three ways. First, his teachers drove by our home while playing "Pomp and Circumstance" from their cars. It was very cool, actually. Second, the school district decided to have seniors drive through campus at designated times, blasting their car horns, and being cheered by teachers, administration, and staff. Third, the superintendent made a bold move by asking families to choose if they wanted a graduation or not. Most—85 percent—said yes, so we had a quick one-hour graduation.

Andrew's graduation was outdoors, and everyone had to wear a mask. No processional, no passing out of programs, no long speeches. Everyone sat or stood six feet apart. Graduation from start to finish was sixty minutes. Sanitizers were everywhere.

The dominant phrase of 2020 and some of 2021 was "social distancing." We had to be six feet apart from others in public, and many states mandated mask wearing. Over the course of six months, we still knew very little about this virus. Schools were in flux, trying to discern how much teaching to do in person and how much to take online. People debated the use of masks.

Meanwhile, I was thrashing internally with stress and feeling socially distant from God.

Where Is God?

"Where is God's voice in all of this global nightmare?" I asked. The pandemic of 2020 helped us acknowledge that we felt out of control. We are humans with limits. We had no answers to the virus. We were all waiting on a vaccine to fix everything. Where was God in all this commotion and confusion? Everyone seemed to be speaking—except God. Why did God seem to be on mute during one of the most excruciating and perplexing times on planet Earth? This was not only a pandemic of sickness; it was a pandemic of *stress*.

The year 2020 brought many voices and lots of noise, pressure, and trauma. This actually continued into 2021 with the coronavirus and the delta variant.

The main voices for every waking moment were the medical world (doctors, infectious disease experts); the WHO (World Health Organization, not the band), news feeds, Twitter, CNN, and Fox news; Facebook, social media, the POTUS, and the FDA. Every day, many voices. Mostly from the government.

Too many talking heads about the what, why, when, and how of the coronavirus.

The book of Romans instructs us to submit to the governing authorities who are "God's servants for your good" (Rom. 13:4). Scripture does say

God *can* speak to and through our leaders (see Proverbs 21:1).

The Bible *never* says God speaks all the time through every president, congresswoman, or governing authorities, but it does tell us to be honor and submit to them because God gave them authority to lead and protect us.

In our day and age, the voices of government, policies, arguments between Democrats and Republicans, racism, sports, and political correctness come to us 24/7 through the media. The only way to disengage is to turn it off. If we don't, we are sure to miss the whisper.

Is God Present or Absent During Stressful Times?

The first detractor and distractor is *stress*. We all face it. Daily. It comes in all shapes and sizes. Stress can be emotional, physical, or spiritual. It might be related to your work. It could be related to a broken relationship. Stress certainly can become a hindrance to hearing God's voice.

Stress makes it hard for many of us to concentrate, which leads us down a dangerous path. We begin to think God is not around. This sometimes leads me to assume that His silence means *He is absent*. Many of the biblical writers had that feeling at times.

As I reflect on the global pandemic and God's apparent absence to many, I have grappled with five big questions concerning God's presence or absence in the midst of stress. Let's unpack those in this chapter.

1. If God is present with us, does that mean He controls all things?

Possibly the most overused phrase in the Christian community during the coronavirus was "God is still in control." Christians are very good at using pat phrases: "God is *still* on the throne" or "God's got this" or "God is in *total* control." I wonder often what those phrases mean. What happens to *your world* when you don't sense *God is in* control of your situation?

What do you *do* when you feel God is not active?" How do you depend on God when you don't know how you are going to pay your next water bill? Maybe you have found yourself singing, "God has never let me down *yet*." What if the *yet* actually happens?

There are some phrases we hear often that the Bible never uses, such as "God won't give you more than you can handle" or "God helps those who help themselves" You will not find them in the Scriptures.

Will you find the phrase "God is in control" in the Bible? Sorry, the answer is no.

Now, before you check out on me, please understand that there are many Scripture verses that speak of God's power and sovereignty. God is called ruler and king. Lord and God. He is the Creator of the universe, stars, and galaxies. We know and believe that God loves us. God is for us and with us. He comes to us in the person of Jesus—God with skin on.

The Bible teaches that God is present everywhere (omnipresent) and is all-knowing (omniscient). C. S. Lewis was known to say, "We may ignore, but we can nowhere evade the presence of God. The world is crowded with Him. He walks everywhere incognito."

In 2020, with all the noise of Covid-19, God's voice seemed to become non-existent at times for many of us. God felt incognito.

I felt the silence of God, and it rattled me.

I *do not believe* God caused and created the coronavirus. It's a virus like the common cold but much worse. I also do not believe that God causes earthquakes, hurricanes, and famines and enjoys watching little kids die. I don't think that God gave cancer to my friend, Derek, who battled it courageously for ten years while thousands prayed for his healing. Then he passed away.

A millennial recently said to me, "If God is controlling all events; He is doing a really *bad* job." I think I understand what he means. "God is in control" does not mean He is behind every detail and event. When I drive a car and keep my hands firmly on the steering wheel, I am in control. If, however, I begin playing with the radio station or want to drive and text on my phone at the same time and end up in a ditch, what happened? I lost control. Whose fault was it? Mine!

Does God control people? Does He manipulate us so we will obey better and faster? No, He does not. We are not puppets on a string.

To suggest "God is *not* in control" sounds like blasphemy or heresy. It feels like we are insulting and disrespecting God. What if God *never* intended to "control" all events, people, and circumstances? We say, "God is in control" perhaps to comfort ourselves, to make ourselves feel better.

Do you really think God created the house fire in which all the family members died? I have trouble swallowing that one. I have seen some people either leave the faith or become disenchanted with Christianity over that crazy thinking. Why? I think it's bad theology to suggest that God orders *all* events.

If God were controlling every outcome, some would say, in baseball terms, "God struck out." Does God determine the outcome of the World Series? Olympics? Super Bowl? Nope.

A number of people have embraced a very extreme, conservative, hyper-Calvinistic approach to life that believes God is on the *control panel* with every episode of life. When a teenager is killed in a car wreck, does that mean God caused it? Was God sleeping and lost focus?

Does God cause you to lose your job, your marriage, your house, your child? Really? When things don't go our way, guess who gets the judging finger pointed at Him? God gets the blame because some believe He not only allowed the cancer, car wreck, or missing child—he sanctioned it. Really?

That is not true. We can be, however, fully confident that even though we live in fallen Babylon, God is for us and with us in the incarnation of Jesus. Better yet, Christ lives *in* us, giving us the hope of glory.

How do we reconcile the control panel of God and His apparent silence?

We don't.

We live in the *tension* of knowing that God knows why. He does things and allows things, and we do not understand them as humans. We leave the mystery to God. God sometimes chooses to limit His power and control. *Most tragedies of life are the result of living in a fallen world.* God does have a plan, but He does not orchestrate or ordain sin. There is no evil in God's nature (see James 1:13).

Does God use and *allow* difficulty for our good? Absolutely! Listen to Paul's popular words in Romans 8:28: "And we know that for those who love God all things work together for good, for those who are called according to his purpose" (ESV).

Paul does not say *all* experiences are good. Not all outcomes are good. Paul states that all things work together *for good* to "those who love God." The idea is that in the midst of hardships and pain, God will use it for our good. Most of us do not read the next verse, which is pivotal in understanding verse 28. In Romans 8:28–29, Paul comments on the previous passage: "...for those who are called according to his purpose. For those whom he foreknew he also predestined to be conformed to the image of his Son, in order that he might be the firstborn among many brothers." brother" (vv. 28-29).

God wants us to love Him, but He will never force us to love Him. We will never fully understand His plans and purposes. God's ultimate goal through life's best and worst is that we come out looking, talking, smelling, and acting *like* Jesus! God's purpose in all things is that we be "conformed not to the world" but transformed by the renewing of our minds to Christ (see Romans 12:2). God's intent is that we be "conformed to the image of his son (Jesus)" by the renewing, not the *removing*, of our minds!

Look like Jesus. Reflect Jesus. And in the midst of silence, trust Jesus. God's goal is to transform us, making us new species of being, new creations (see 2 Corinthians 5:17). Old things are passing away. All things are becoming new.

2. How does God's silence impact us in a fallen world?

Nothing surprises God; He allows things to happen because He knows all things. It's called *foreknowledge*. He knows what is going to happen. He knows the reasons and the outcome. As humans, we might see the outcomes of situations, but we don't know the *why* and *how* of these scenarios. Let's not pretend that we know.

I prefer the word "allow" rather than "cause" when it comes to divine movement and God's "control." I have preached at more than thirty-five funerals, and most of them were very difficult to navigate for the loved ones. Some situations were gut-wrenching.

The first funeral I officiated was for a twenty-five-year-old who had committed suicide. The second funeral was for a five-year-old who died of spina bifida. I have preached at four funerals for people who died as a result of suicide, one from a car wreck, and others so tragic that I kept hearing parents ask the most difficult question to answer: "Why, God?"

How cruel would it be for any pastor to tell the parent of a child who dies of cancer that "the Lord *killed* your child" or "The Lord needed another angel in heaven"? Some pastors try to soften the blow by saying, "The Lord took your son or daughter." Grieving parents cannot wrap their minds around losing a child. As parents, we think our kids are meant to outlive us, not die before us.

God can do whatever He wants. I get it. Let's stop assuming that we know what's behind His will. Maybe you've heard the song "He's Got the Whole World in His Hands." If God took His hands off the control panel of the solar system, it would implode, right? At the same time, God *can* control anything He wants and chooses, but there are times when I believe He takes his hands *off* the panel. These ambiguities cause all kinds of hurt, heartaches, and doubts concerning whether God is good or not. This is not just an issue for non-Jesus followers; it's an issue for most people of faith.

I believe the world God created has derailed because we humans seem to enjoy breaking God's laws and principles. We live in a world of sin and brokenness. We choose to violate God's ways.

At the same time, nothing that happens on planet Earth gets past God's knowledge. Some theologians refer to this as the "permissive will of God." It's the idea that God *permits or allows* certain things to happen rather than causes it. His sovereignty means God knows everything that is going to happen. He knows us. He cares and loves us.

What we do know from the Genesis narrative is that God gave the first humans authority over the Earth, both pre-fall and post-fall (sin). Adam was given *control* over all things: "Fill the earth and subdue it. Rule over the fish in the sea and over the birds in the sky and over every living creature that moves on the ground" (Gen. 1:28). Then God said, "I give you every seed-bearing plant on the face of the whole earth, and every tree that has fruit with seed in it" (Gen. 1:29–30).

God allows evil, cancers, and hurricanes, but He is not responsible for creating them. Evil hearts do evil things. There are natural and ecological calamities. God can do anything He wants to because He is God, but He limits himself in controlling *all* things. God does not drive my car, He does not fix my breakfast, and He does not run errands for me. He does not fix my plumbing. God has given *us responsibilities* for His planet. We manage it. We are his stewards.

Life happens. All people, godly, or evil, will get sick and die. No one is exempt. Life. Death. Paying taxes.

The reason I struggle with the word "control" as it relates to God's voice is because it's another word for *manipulation*—and that is not God's agenda. Love is not about control or forcing someone to do something. Love and manipulation are diametrically opposed to each other. A "controlling" parent might be viewed as abusive in our culture. Love and control are antithetical. Incompatible. Control is about mistreating, exploiting people. Jesus was never about doing that. He encourages people to follow Him, and He allows people to walk away from Him. Jesus never coerces folks to come back.

Manipulation, control, and power are about cruelty, not love. True love from God allows us to make decisions, and we learn to live with our choices, regrets, and consequences. Jesus is the Good Shepherd, and shepherds lead and guide their sheep. Sometimes, the sheep stay with the shepherd; other times, they roam and get lost. I love the phrase in Psalm 23:2 (ESV), "He *leads* us besides still waters"—it doesn't say "He *makes* or *forces* us to come to the waters."

My professor friend, Ben, says, "God has the ability of taking control at any time or anyplace *if* and *when* He wants to. God has the right to control anything and everything. He has the control panels right in front of Him—He just doesn't always *take* control." In other words, sometimes God limits His influence over the control panel.

As finite as we humans are, the real issue is that we do not know *why* He does and doesn't do things. We do not know what He determines at times. What we do know is that God gives us a great and mysterious gift. It's two words: *free will*—in other words, *the power of choice*. God has given us the ability to make decisions. We have to live with the outcomes. What I do know is this: humans like control, and maybe God is telling us to let go of what we cannot control.

Our choices matter, even when it seems God is absent.

Very few people decide at an early age to screw up their lives. All of us start with a clean slate at birth. Somehow, on the road of life, we choose wisely or go the way of perdition. Not too many intentionally decide to mess up their marriage, their finances, or their kids.

All of us have made poor decisions. And most of us have avoided bad conclusions because of wise decision making.

Life is about decision making. We have to live with the consequences of our choices. And we have to live with those decisions, one conclusion at a time. Decisions impact our direction. Choices lead to developing our character. Decisions lead to our destination.

Your choices impact everything. What will the outcomes be if you don't lean on God, or pray very little, or let the dust on your Bible grow? God *never* makes me pray. I choose to sometimes. God does not make me mentor people. He does not strong-arm me to share my Christian faith. It's all about choices. Free will is powerful.

And when I watch TV, I am choosing *that* over other things.

Maybe one day I choose a lot of social media over reading God's Word. God does not strike me down. The day I spend more time in prayer doesn't mean I won't get indigestion or a rash on my face.

Our choices can change many outcomes.

What decision do you need to make when it comes to *your* pandemic of stress?

3. Does stress play into the fact that God seems absent and we can end up missing Him in the moment?

The answer is a resounding yes! Sometimes God is silent because He chooses to be silent. He does not need to speak every minute, like Twitter feeds or other social media. God does not have to speak unless He wants or needs to.

In the Bible, we see words like "The Lord says," so we believe that God does speak to people. In fact, many people today wish God would speak to them more frequently. I certainly do.

Sometimes, God uses His silence to drive us to our knees to seek Him when we have been running away or just plain too busy to stop the madness. God uses silence to draw us in.

God can use stress in our lives because He wants us to take risks, to leap, and to discern things. God wants us to use our sanctified imaginations and intelligence.

We can miss God when we are stressed out.

Consider the two narratives mentioned in John 20 and 21 that illustrate this. Jesus has risen from the dead, and the disciples—as many times as they heard from Jesus that He would rise from the dead—still did not believe Him (See John 20:9). In fact, Mark's Gospel records that Jesus told His disciples that the "Son of Man" would be killed and three days later would rise. "But they did not understand the saying, and were afraid to ask him" (Mark 9:32, ESV).

This was a stressful time for the followers of Jesus.

Mary Magdalene, who began following Jesus after she had been delivered from demon oppression, went to the empty tomb. She began to cry, and two angels asked her, "Why are you crying?" Mary believed that the body of Jesus had been taken away. She did not understand that He had risen from the dead. Now watch the next line. It grips me with honest hope and authenticity: "At this, she turned around and saw Jesus standing there, but she did not realize that it was Jesus" (John 20:14).

Jesus was right in front of Mary, yet she did not see him. She missed him—that is, until He spoke her name, "Mary." She knew that voice, the voice of her shepherd. The Good Shepherd. She ran back to tell the news of the risen Christ to the disciples.

Jesus said, "My sheep know my voice." Her eyes were opened. Her ears were unplugged.

In John 21, Jesus again appeared to the disciples by the Sea of Galilee. Peter was in the midst of stress and discouragement, disoriented by the happenings of the week. So he returned to his old vocation of fishing. He and a few disciples fished all night and came up empty-handed: "Early in the morning, Jesus stood on the shore, but the disciples did not realize that it was Jesus" (John 21:4).

For the second time in two chapters, Jesus was right in their midst, but they did not see Him. Now, don't you feel better about your own spiritual life? Aren't you glad John the disciple included this in the Bible? Maybe now you won't feel so alone in your ability to hear and see Jesus.

After Jesus told the young men where to throw their nets, they hit the jackpot and caught 153 fish. The disciples then recognized Jesus. Like Mary, it was when they heard His voice.

"Come and have breakfast," Jesus said. I love this next line: "None of the disciples dared ask him, 'Who are you?' They knew it was the Lord" (John 21:12, NLT). After these resurrection appearances, the disciples actually saw Jesus. It took time; it was a process. For doubting Thomas, it took a real physical touch of Jesus's broken body—His hands and feet— for Thomas to believe, see, and understand.

It's easy to miss Jesus, isn't it? Stress has a way of blinding us from seeing Him.

4. In my stressful situations, shouldn't I focus more on how to respond than on why it's happening?

Most of us want to know the reason *why* we are facing stress and difficulty, yet we will be dejected if we focus solely on the "why." Both the why and how are vital. Often, the *why* can answer the *how*. Let's say you are stressed about school. It's important to fix the problem. You are not sleeping well. We should ask, "Why the lack of sleep?"

If the answer is, "I'm drinking lots of coffee at night," then we know one of the ways to resolve it—limit the coffee! You have now addressed the why and how of the stress. Or maybe the source of a student's stress is not understanding calculus and losing sleep at night. In that case, one solution is to find a tutor.

Sometimes, life is easy to figure out; other times, not so much. There will be times none of us will know why things are happening in our lives.

God knows where we are going to live and die and when we will die. God knows our life span. He knows what we like, why we choose certain hobbies or sports teams, and why we like chocolate and dislike okra and green beans from a can.

When life gets stressful, we have all kinds of options. We can binge-watch Netflix. God won't outshout it. We can drown ourselves in alcohol. We can overeat or exercise excessively. We can run away from people. We can hide from God. There are many possibilities when life clamps down on us.

Rather than getting *more stressed* out trying to discover *why* we are in the midst of stress, let's alter the storyline and ask God, "Lord, how do you want me to respond? What should my attitude be?"

Once you get a handle on why things might be going downward, then you can focus more on *what to do* about the stress. That will recenter you with God's Spirit and lessen the frustrations.

5. Isn't the point of God's silence more about us decluttering our lives so we can hear His voice?

Absolutely! God gives us the freedom to do right, and He even allows us to make poor decisions. God gives us the power to choose. God makes available his Spirit, but we must choose to let the Spirit guide us. Even Jesus chose to obey the Father——he was not pushed into it. Jesus, although fully God and fully man, had to learn obedience (see Hebrews 5:8).

God can take our poor choices, our lousy impulse control, and still transform us. Following Jesus is a mixture of God's Spirit wooing us and our human choice. Deciding to stay in the faith is a combination of God's Spirit and our free will.

Following Jesus has many options. We can read the Bible or cut the grass. We can watch NFL football or go kayaking. Pray or read a novel? Which will bring me closer to God? Well, it depends on the day. Sometimes I get more out of nature than the Bible, and other times, the Scriptures overwhelm me with God's presence.

Find ways to use the gift of "choice" to listen to God's will, to declutter your soul so you can hear the Shepherd's voice.

During the pandemic, many of us felt sequestered in our homes and neighborhood. For a period of weeks, Rhonda and I were scared to venture out into the public domain. We had so many choices concerning how to use our time. One day, we started to notice that our closets, living room, dining room, bedroom, and garage had grown in abundance of junk.

We became pack rats. Not hoarders, but it was getting close. We decided to gather our stuff into three piles—keep, give away, and throw away. It became freeing as I made dozens of trips to the local dump and local Goodwill. Slowly but surely, we got liberated from a lot of stuff. As we began the purging process, I had an epiphany: Part of the learning process during the pandemic was more than decluttering my personal possessions; *it was about decluttering my soul!*

One of the great values of being a Christian is that as I become more like Jesus. I choose to *imitate* Jesus. So I sometimes choose to fast during the year (although I would rather eat); I choose to have solitude in prayer (although my flesh would rather watch college football). As I grow in Christ, I learn a valuable lesson: God allows me some diversions in life. Jesus was not always teaching and preaching. He hiked, took naps, fished, and ate food, like everyone else.

We are not very good at governing and "controlling" our lives. I am a horrible god, so I ask His Spirit to lead me. I move from "For me to live is me" to "for me to live is Christ!" This is not an overnight makeover. *It is a daily process.* It takes time. And I began to declutter my inner world.

God's Silence Can Be Confusing

When national disasters like hurricanes, forest fires, or the coronavirus happen, it creates so much confusion. What can we learn from these tragedies?

In her book called *Everything Happens for a Reason: And Other Lies I've Loved*, Kate Bowler describes her journey with stage IV colon cancer. She likes to say in interviews, "Everything happens! That is, it—everything—happens. Period."[1]

If "everything happens for a reason" is accurate, then the question becomes, "What is the reason for this?" The answer is, most of us don't know and might never know. What we do know is this: God asks us to look to Him, to simplify our lives, and to get our souls connected to the One who made us.

Let's ask God for His help, His clarity, and His love. He will always give us free will. Some days, you will feel ecstatic because you sense the presence of God. Other days will be just ordinary.

Let me give you a piece of advice: just move on to the next day. Stress will be there waiting for you at some level, guaranteed. Take a deep breath. Don't freak out over the possibility of missing God's voice or His will. Times of stress are normative. Not hearing God's voice is not always a deal breaker. Stressors will come and go. Stress is a distractor, but it doesn't have to defeat us.

If you miss it today, so what? Take the pressure off yourself. You are not God. There is always tomorrow to start over. Learn ways to let the stress go. Listen for God's whisper.

Make the choice. Each day.

---

1. Kate Bowler, *Everything Happens for a Reason: And Other Lies I've Loved* (New York: Random House, 2019).

Big Takeaway: Stress is a distractor. Make wise choices to alleviate stress. Stress will definitely get in your way. Pay attention to the tension of stress. Learn how to enter silence.

Questions for Reflection

1. What is your reaction to Dr. Olshine's concept that God does not rule every detail of life? Do you agree or disagree? Why?
2. How do you view God's control and sovereignty?
3. When suffering happens, how do you think God is involved or not involved?
4. What are some of the issues in life that make you question whether God is running the planet's affairs—especially your own?
5. In what specific ways do you need to ask God to help reduce the stress you are facing?

CHAPTER SEVEN

I DOUBT IT: CAN FAITH AND DOUBT COEXIST?

"Doubt is a state of mind in suspension between faith and unbelief."
—Os Guinness

L ife is risky.

A few years ago, I had a speaking engagement in Charleston, South Carolina. Charleston is one of my favorite cities in the United States. We asked the church if they would be willing to cover an extra night at the hotel so we could relax an extra day and get in some beach time. They graciously agreed.

We went to the beach called Isle of Palms, a gorgeous setting of sun and sand and water. We hung out for several hours, playing on the beach, body surfing, and snacking. Following lunch, we ventured out into the waves, when suddenly my wife started shouting at the top of her lungs, "Shark! Shark! Shark!"

There had to be at least one hundred people around us, and nobody budged. No one moved.

Then Rhonda got louder: "*Shark, shark…David, Andrew, get out!*" (At this point, my wife did not care about the other folks—just her men.)

With much exhortation and emphasis, I said to my son, Andrew (as you remember, Andrew has Down syndrome, and was turning eighteen years old at the time), "We need to get out of the water!"

"Why?" he asked.

"Because there is a shark."

Andrew said, "But I *love* sharks!"

It is true that my son really does love sharks, and Andrew is an animal expert, more than anyone I know. He owns probably one thousand animal books.

I told Andrew now was *not* the time to love sharks! We finally got out of the water. We sat on the beach for about an hour, and then we got back in the water when we thought the coast was clear.

Why did we get back in the waves? Because we love the ocean and because life is *risky*. Yes, we swim in the ocean with the knowledge that there are stingrays out there (I have experienced their powerful sting on my right foot), jellyfish (been stung by them, too), sea urchins (check), as well as sharks and other predators (which I gratefully have avoided). We still go out there. My friend, Julian, says, "If you knew what was really out there, you would not go out there!"

We still go out there, knowing fully well we're in enemy territory.

Life involves *risk taking*. Almost every day, I get into my car, fully aware that any at moment, I could be in a crash. Driving a car is risky, and I have been in an accident or two in my life to prove it, but I got back in. And I still do drive a car regularly.

Life has risks. So does faith, and where there is faith, doubt is lurking in the backseat.

If there was ever a subject that can divert us from missing God's voice, it is doubt. Faith is risky because it has a cousin named doubt, and it can mess with our ability to listen well and get quiet. Doubt brings a lot of noise to our minds.

What Is Doubt?

The Oxford dictionary defines *doubt* as a "feeling of uncertainty or lack of conviction." Doubt is that place between trust and disbelief. Doubt has been given a bad rap in the world of Christianity. Some have the idea that doubt is the "unpardonable sin," yet I believe it is an essential part of the journey of faith.

My buddy and fellow professor, Dr. Larry Wagner, were having breakfast one early morning in a restaurant. We were discussing faith and doubt. Wagner (aka "Wags") said to me, "'A faith without some doubts isn't a deep faith."

I agree. He's saying that if you have some doubts, you have faith! We talked about how many of the college and graduate students we work with have believed the lie that they are not allowed to question their faith. Wags said to me, "Basically, if you wrestle with faith, that's a pretty strong indicator that you have one."

Faith and doubt coexist.

Dominic Done is a pastor and fellow struggler with doubts. He writes, "Doubts are normal. You doubt because you are human. Because we live in a world of limits, we doubt. Doubt isn't a destination but a road to be traveled. God loves doubters. The Bible is full of them. Doubts are normal. We doubt because we are human."[1]

"God loves doubters."

The Bible speaks of this in the one-chapter New Testament book called Jude. Verse 22 says, "Be merciful to those who doubt."

If you do not believe me, listen to a man who was not prepared to lose his child, whose situation looked bleak and hopeless. The father brings his tormented son to Jesus, asking Him to heal him: "And Jesus said to him, 'If you can. All things are possible for one who believes.' Immediately the father of the child cried out and said, 'I believe, help my *unbelief*'" (Mark 9:23–24, ESV).

Notice the words side by side uttered by a desperate dad: "I believe… help my unbelief."

Faith and doubt together. Doubt is swinging between yes and no, believe and unbelief. Jesus did not reprimand or insult the man for his comment, "Help my unbelief." Instead, Jesus healed the boy.

Why Do People Doubt?

Every year, we see a number of leaders, speakers, entertainers, musicians, and mega-church pastors walk away from the church, or even the faith. What causes this departure? Why do people doubt when it comes to faith issues? I believe we can boil it down to a few key reasons: Suffering, Scripture, science, and speculation. Let's look at each of these stumbling blocks.

---

1. Dominic Done, *When Faith Fails: Finding God in the Shadow of Doubt* (Nashville, Thomas Nelson, 2019), 10–11.

1. Suffering

Connie lost both her parents in a car wreck. Ethan's brother died of leukemia. Andy experienced a traumatic divorce. Did I mention that life can be cruel and brutal? Ever since these difficult losses, each person has struggled with believing God is around. Can you blame them?

As Bono of the band U2 sang, "The stars are bright, but do they know? The universe is beautiful but cold."

The apostle Paul knew storms, suffering, and shipwrecks. When we see someone abandon the faith, Paul called it being "shipwrecked." He describes two men in 1 Timothy 1:18–19, Hymenaeus and Alexander, who "have made shipwreck of their faith" (ESV). Some folks believe and come back. Some leave altogether. Peter had a stormy and rocky life, proclaimed to speak up for Jesus, then denied Jesus, yet later became of the greatest leaders of the early church. Judas believed Jesus, then turned his back on Him, only to take his own life for being a traitor.

Suffering is perhaps the biggest reason why people struggle with doubts. We all live in a fallen world with daily difficulties and tragedies. Suffering results when we wrestle with the question, "Why does God allow evil?"

Storms and suffering are unsettling.

Some have suggested that suffering would not be a problem if there was *no God*, but when you bring into the equation the existence of God, the reality of suffering becomes, in some ways, more troublesome. English Anglican priest David Watson was famous for saying, "Suffering *only* becomes a problem when we accept the existence of God."

A young man named Will has talked to me for years about how he has prayed for his alcoholic dad to be free from his addiction, but there is no change. Leticia prays that her parents will become Christians, but there seems to be no movement. A mom in my city lives with the daily exhaustion of knowing that her daughter was killed during her second year of college, and the murderer has never been found. She has lost all hope and belief in God.

The world can be awesome, beautiful, and horrible. And when people suffer, perhaps the biggest doubt emerges: "I wonder if God speaks at all?"

2. Scripture

Not only do we see prominent Christians leaving the faith; some leave their marriages. One of these persons said, "I'm genuinely losing my faith, and it doesn't bother me."

What is behind this? What causes this? Sometimes it's the Bible.

You will hear it often: "Why is the Bible full of contradictions?" *Fundamentalism* has not helped. Not everything in the Bible is meant to be read in a literal way. And abusing the Bible and some of those verses has historically been a problem. Many preachers' dogmatic opinions have sent people marching out of the church.

Poor interpretation of the Bible can hurt people's faith. Those who read the Bible with great scrutiny will find passages that are upsetting, and that can turn the tide from faith to doubts.

3. Science

Besides suffering and Scripture, science has caused lots of trouble and skepticism for some. There has been the ongoing debate for years over the creation narrative. Is it meant to be literal or symbolic? Can one believe in faith *and* evolution? Is the Earth young (thousands of years), or is it old (millions of years)? No matter what you believe about science, it has created a thorny issue for some people of the faith.

Are faith and science compatible?

Cannot the two meet, or do they have to remain polar opposites?

4. Speculation

Every denomination was founded with a particular teaching or doctrine. These areas can cause a spark of interest or create controversy. Here are some issues that have been around for a while, with some gaining traction:

- How do we interpret sexual and gender orientations?
- What is the role of women in the church?
- Do spiritual gifts all exist, or did some cease at the end of the apostolic age?
- Can you lose your salvation, or is it "Once saved, always saved"?
- Is hell a scorcher? Are the eternal fire and damnation of hell literal or imagery?
- Do I have to be baptized to go to heaven?

Recently, Alex, a millennial, said to me, "The way my friends describe what they think the Bible means for those who do not follow Jesus, means my dad, mom, brother, cousins, and most of my best friends will be punished in fire and brimstone for all of eternity. This is a mean and cruel God. How could I believe in an abusive God like that?"

My friend, Tony Campolo, calls issues that create doubt "hot potatoes."

- What about people like Hitler, Mussolini, and Ben Laden… will they go to heaven if they pray the "sinner's prayer" as they approach death?
- Some people teach universal salvation as biblical, right? *Universalism* means all will go to heaven. What do you think about that teaching?
- What about the teachings of *annihilation* (God judges all people, and then the believer receives heaven, and the nonbeliever is destroyed and gets no eternal punishment)?
- Can a Christian watch certain TV shows and movies?
- Should Christian preachers talk about politics and social issues?

All these ideas, concepts, and "doctrines" can make people's heads spin. They can be unsettling. Racial reconciliation, the Confederate flag, loyalty to the government, use of guns, abortion, passivism, and other controversial issues cause many people's blood pressure to rise. They can create factions, worry, distrust, and doubt.

I have seen people leave the church over the choice of the carpet for the sanctuary. I've seen people leave the faith over hell, women's roles, LGBTQ, and music. Teaching is too long. Too Wesleyan. Too charismatic. Too reformed. No application. Too *dispensational* (look that word up). I never hear complaints about the sermon being too short. Just saying.

Then people get all fussy over music. Yes, music styles are a lightning rod for many: "Too loud." "Too contemporary." "Too soft." "Too traditional." "What is this, a Rolling Stones concert?" "That lead singer cannot carry a tune."

More than doctrines or teachings that rattle people's cages, the main reason folks leave the church or the faith is *relationships*. Relational conflicts create doubt.

Speculation creates doubts, and doubt produces pain, depression, hurt, loneliness, and confusion. It also is a gateway to growth and hope. I am a doubter about some things that come with the Christian faith. I have serious doubts about some preachers' theologies and soap boxes. I certainly have major doubts when some claim that if people have faith, they will be pain-free. Doubt is a huge distractor and detractor.

Hebrews 13:9 states, "Don't be lured away from him by the latest *speculations* about him" (MSG).

"Some Doubted"

The good news is that God affirms those with questions and doubt. Doubt is not bad. Doubt can be a powerful tool to draw us deeper into the life of the Spirit.

After Jesus's resurrection, we see the disciples standing with Jesus: "When they saw him, they worshiped him; but some *doubted*" (Matt. 28:17).

"Some doubted." Isn't that amazing?

Aren't you glad that verse was recorded in the Bible? I mean, how could the disciples who spent three years with Jesus, now standing next to the risen Jesus, still doubt?

"I believe; help my unbelief."

How could Matthew write, "Some doubted" in the Bible? Will it not discredit Christianity? The answer is no, it will not—actually, it will *validate* the faith. As a fellow struggler with doubt, I love the honesty of the Scriptures.

Worshipping doubters at the resurrection. Doubting worshippers. The disciples are doing both at the same time.

If you are one who struggles with any kind of doubt, you probably have asked these kinds of questions. I insist, please keep asking them:

- Does God really exist?
- Why does God not intervene in my situation when I have prayed like crazy?
- Did the resurrection of Jesus really happen?
- Did I make up all this faith stuff in my head?

Doubts are really part of our DNA. Doubt and faith are woven into our being. You are not weird or lacking in faith because you have questions, curiosity, and doubts. Doubt does not need to be your adversary. Allow it to be your ally.

Can't we let people honestly struggle without putting more quilt trips on them? Doubt is confusing and unsettling and messy and mind-boggling and beautiful and powerful.

Doubts forces a reaction and some kind of decision. It confuses us emotionally, intellectually, and spiritually. Doubt is messy and mind-boggling. There have been times, when it comes to faith and doubt, I have felt like I needed a few sessions with a clinical counselor who has multiple degrees in psychology, philosophy, and theology and a whole lot of compassion!

What is so frustrating about faith and doubt?

Sometimes people feel so overwhelmed with intellectual or spiritual questions that it can cause them to just throw up their hands and quit.

It can create more questions than answers.

Some Implications for the Marathon

Reconciling faith and doubt is not a sprint, it's a marathon. It's not about speed, it's about endurance. I believe there are four practical implications as we wrestle with the detractor of doubt.

1. Understand that reconciling faith and doubt is about packing your own bags.

If you have doubts, you will eventually *wrestle* with God if you want to be a player in the realm of faith. Your doubts will always lead you somewhere. And don't be afraid of the tension or the paradox. It is there to keep us moving, growing, questioning, and resolving. Doubt is sometimes a crisis.

I meet some folks who say they never have doubts. Good for them. I've discovered, however, that is not most people's experiences.

God uses faith and doubt to change us.

As a youth pastor, I have seen many kids and teens growing up in the church abandon or wander from the faith. Some do so because, well, maybe they never had a personal faith to begin with. I would rather err on the side of believing that many students were holding onto the coattails of the faith of their parents, siblings, or friends. My friend, Fran, calls teenage faith "affiliation faith." Affiliation faith is about "who is going on the retreat." Young people want to know which friends are going to the camp. Many of them could not care less who the speaker is or what band is playing. It's a faith based on friendships.

There is nothing wrong with a faith involving friends, unless that is your only anchor. Until the faith is personalized and galvanized, it is a faith that has the chance of drowning.

It's kind of up to you. Do the hard work of personally analyzing and claiming faith as your own. Personal ownership is part of the elixir.

If you do, not only will you own it, nobody can take your faith away!

Going to summer camp in Wisconsin was the highlight of my life growing up. Each year, as time to go to camp was approaching, my mom would begin her regular routine of packing my bags. She would sew my name into all my clothes, including my underwear. It got kind of embarrassing.

My mom is great. Each year, she continued to pack my bags for the summer camp of six weeks.

My last year of camp, I was turning thirteen, so I wanted to be more like a man than a kid. I wanted to feel like a grown-up. As we were getting ready for camp, I went into my bedroom one afternoon, and my mom was doing her thing.

I said, "Hey, what are you doing?"

"I am packing your stuff."

I became a little louder and said, "Nope, nope. No more!"

She looked at me and asked, "Why not?"

I said, "It's time for *me* to pack my own bags."

My mom got the message.

I think she was trying to get me to that point all along. She was preparing me for that moment. It was like my mom was waiting for this *ownership* to happen years ago, and probably should have, but I was not ready. I think she walked out of my bedroom with a smirk on her face.

Isn't that what God is after with us, to get us ready to pack our own spiritual bags so we can listen better to His voice?

God's goal is for us to encounter Him, but it will take some discipline on our part to pull out the suitcase and start packing our faith bags. God is leading us to that point. Let your doubts drive you toward more faith. Feed your faith, not just your doubts.

Let the detractor of doubt lead to becoming the attractor to the faith.

2. Be prepared for some pain.

Meet someone I think you will like. His name is Jacob, and he is one of my favorite characters in the Bible. Jacob was the son of Isaac and Rebecca and the grandson of Abraham. Jacob was cunning and deceitful, especially toward his twin brother, Esau.

Jacob struggled with faith and doubt. I identify with him, for he wrestled with God. And when God takes us into battles of doubt, there is a small price to pay. It results in some pain. The pain of change is sometimes harder than the pain of staying the same. Jacob learned this the *hard way.*

Jacob was a child of the covenant. He also had a doubt problem. He wondered, "Can I trust God?"

Genesis 28 chronicles Jacob's journey to Haran. He stops for the night because it is past sundown. He lies down in the dark and falls asleep. Jacob has a dream of a stairway from Earth to heaven. (I don't think Led Zeppelin's song "Stairway to Heaven" came from this narrative.)

When Jacob awakes, he says, "Surely the presence of the Lord was here, and I was *unaware* of it" (Gen. 28:16).

This might be one of the most profound sayings in the Bible, and I totally relate with it. I have been in many situations (none like Jacob with angels and ladders, though). Looking back, I had no idea what God was up to. Hindsight is 20/20.

I was not cognizant of His presence or voice. Can I get a witness?

Group hug.

Following this narrative, Jacob ends up meeting God, or a divine being.

They go to the wrestling mat and start sweating and scrapping with each other. Jacob wrestles with God all night long, and his thigh is ripped out of socket. God wins. Not a fair fight. With all the sweating, huffing and puffing, aching, and pounding of muscles, this is more than a physical fight. It is a spiritual war of faith versus doubt: "The sun came up as he (Jacob) left Peniel, limping because of his hip. That is why Israelites to this day don't eat the hip muscle, because Jacob's hip was thrown out of joint" (Gen. 32:31–32, MSG).

Jacob was struggling. He walked away with a limp. The question is, are you and I willing to go to the mat with God? Are we ready to rumble?

When doubt and faith meet each other head-on in battle, there will be hardship, heartache, and some bruises along the way. Doubt often feels like a huge loss. I felt this when Andrew was born. I just did not know why God gave us this kid and what exactly we were to do with him, other than just love him and take care of him. The climb to the top of the mountain of raising a special-needs kid was emotionally excruciating, to say the least. The doubts piled up like fall leaves in my backyard!

Rarely does an athlete come away unbruised and pain-free. No pain, no gain.

That is why we love the Olympics—the hard work, discipline, and stress that took these athletes years to develop is remarkable and inspiring.

Non-athletes probably don't appreciate all the years of blood, sweat, and tears, wins and defeats, discouragements and victories that come with the territory.

When faith and doubt meet head-on, it is identical to a wrestling match. Jacob ends up having a life-changing experience. God changed his name from Jacob to Israel.

As you wrestle with whether faith and doubt can coexist, just consider this: if you learn to pack your own spiritual bags, and you limp off in pain, then I have good news for you: your faith is deeper than you thought.

3. Be brutally honest.

My hope is that you will not jump ship, but hang in there long enough to be real. So many characters in the Scriptures wrestled with faith and doubt. They were ruthlessly vulnerable and authentic with God. If you don't believe me, just read the books of Psalms and Lamentations.

Be honest with God about all the things you think and feel. He can handle all your questions and skepticism. Let's give all doubters a break, okay? Give them some friendly space to breathe and question things.

Is doubt bugging you? Doubt does not have to be an enemy. It can be your friend.

Austin Fischer writes, "I don't have to fear my doubts…Most of the people I've seen walk away from faith are not those who expressed doubt but those who refused to express their doubts until it was too late…"[2]

True.

I have met way too many Gen X and Gen Y folks who waited years to deal with their doubts. Fisher encourages us that whatever we are thinking or feeling, we need to be ruthlessly candid and direct with God:

> Christians tell the truth and tell it to God and the church should be the most honest place in the world…I haven't made many explicit vows to God in my life, but one vow I have made…never to think something about God that I don't also say to God. If I think it, I will pray it. I will tell God about how I feel about God. I will give my doubts no quarter. I will always keep the conversation going. If I crash and burn, I will go down telling God the truth.[3]

One song brings it home for me—"Bigger than I Thought" by Sean Curran. A few lines caught my attention: "Speak to me when the silence steals my voice. You understand me…So I throw all my cares before You. My doubts and fears don't scare you. You're bigger than I thought you were…I believe, help my unbelief…You understand me. I will rest in the Father's hands…"[4]

4. Look for the light in the darkness.

Following Andrew's birth, I went through the normal ebb and flows of hope and despair. I have rarely battled depression, but there was a week or so that I hit a wall, which felt more like falling into a dark hole.

Andrew was about ten weeks old, and Rhonda wanted to go to the mall. I am not a mall guy, but my pastor told me once, "You do things *out of love.*" It takes a lot of *love* to get me to venture out to the mall, so we went.

A major epiphany was about to happen around the corner.

After I had pushed Andrew in his stroller for about twenty minutes. I

2. Austin Fischer, Faith in the Shadows: *Finding Christ in the Midst of Doubt* (Westmont, Illinois: InterVarsity Press, 2018), 35.
3. Ibid., 36–37.
4. Natalie Sims, Sean Curran, and Allen Swoope, "Bigger than I Thought," Musixmatch.

asked Rhonda to watch him because I needed to find a restroom. Within a minute or two, another man came to the urinal next to me. Now, ladies, you might not know this, but there is an unwritten rule, sort of a guy "code," that in a public restroom, you keep your eyes straight ahead and stare at the wall until you have finished your business.

If you peek to your right or left, it is considered intrusive and invasive.

But I could not ignore what was going on next to me. The man, probably in his mid- to late fifties, was in a wheelchair, moaning and groaning. I continued to look ahead at the wall and then asked, "Are you okay?"

"No, I need help."

"What is the issue?" I asked.

I could tell by the way he was speaking slowly that he had some kind of special needs.

"I pooped in my pants," he said.

I was thinking, "I am not going to help this guy in any way. I could end up in jail."

"What do you want me to do?" I asked?

He said, "Can you pull my pants up? My helper is outside and will take care of me when we get home."

I looked around because I was feeling pretty uncomfortable in that moment. I washed my hands, took a deep breath, and complied with the man's request. He thanked me, and I left.

I found Rhonda in the mall. I began to cry.

"My, that was some bathroom experience," Rhonda stated.

"You have no idea," I said.

"What's wrong?" she asked.

"I almost missed it. There was a man with disabilities in the men's bathroom who needed my help. In the past, I would have not only ignored him; I would have not 'seen him.' He would have been, in some ways, invisible to me in the past. But because of having Andrew, the light clicked on in my own darkness."

I saw the man and his needs. Without Andrew in our lives, I would have missed the moment.

Light came into my *dark* place. I did not need a lot of light—just enough to get me through some of the pain.

Since that time, I cannot ignore people with special needs. That moment gave me purpose and insight for the journey of faith, doubt, and God's silence. *He speaks through all kinds of experiences—yes, even in mall bathrooms.*

Light peeked into my darkness.

When Andrew was born, I wondered initially how I would live with him. Now I cannot imagine life without Andrew. He helped me see things for the first time in my life. My eyes were opened.

I see people with disabilities everywhere. I can no longer ignore them. I began to see a new purpose for my life.

Over the years, as Andrew got older, he started competing in athletic venues. He won many Special Olympics events in swimming, tennis, and paddleboarding. We have been involved in Special Olympics since Andrew was a little kid.

He was the only teen with special needs on the local middle and high-school teams for six years, and his team cheered him on with great passion: "Smitty! Smitty! Smitty!" they would chant his nickname.

I now look back to those early days of Andrew's life.

Light broke in a man's restroom that day. God helped me turn some of my doubts into dancing!

Suddenly, it made more sense to me why God gave us a special-needs child. I now see.

In the same way, in your darkest moments filled with doubt, *look for the light*, even the tiniest one. Belief is the small light that can break into the darkness of doubt in the strangest of moments.

King David wrote, "Answer me, oh Lord my God; give me light in my darkness, lest I die" (Ps. 13:3, TLB).

Light in my darkness.

We need to have eyes to see. As Scripture says, "Then he (Jesus) *opened* their minds" (Luke 24:45).

In your darkest moments, filled with doubt, God wants to shed a small light into your world to give you a future and hope. Darkness can feel frightening. It's not easy to see what God is up to. Years later after Andrew's birth, I was able to sing this about him: "God gave me you for the ups and downs, God gave me you for the days of doubts. For when I think I've lost my way, there are no words here left to say, it's true, God gave me you."[5]

The great reformer, Martin Luther, knew doubt. It was his dark night of the soul. Luther struggled with many unanswered questions and ended up penning the great hymn, "A Mighty Fortress Is Our God." That hymn, borne out of darkness and emotional pain, has helped millions of people.

The darkness of doubt can burst forth with new light and hope. Look for the tiny light in the cracks. As Mike Donehey's song "All Together" says, "Can I tell you the state I'm in? Cracks are where the light gets in. Maybe we don't have to have it all together. What if grace made it safe to tell you the truth? Am I the only one who wrestles with doubt? And if I tell you all my secrets, will you go running out? There's only one way to find out."[6]

We all brawl with some kind of doubt. Look for the cracks.

Altar Call?

It would be easy to say, "If you want to get rid of *all* your doubt, give it to Jesus, and within minutes it will be resolved and go away."

I wish that were true.

Rather than that approach, what if I asked you two questions:

1. Are you willing to ask the big questions that nobody is asking and to look for some answers?
2. Will you allow doubt to propel your faith to move out of "shallow waters" into deeper intimacy with Jesus?

I dare you—go for it. Watch what happens.

Big Takeaway: When you allow faith and doubt to coexist, there's a great chance you will develop personal ownership of your faith. It will become yours. And that's worth some pain.

---

5. Blake Shelton and Dave Barnes, "God Gave Me You," 2011, Musixmatch, No Gang Music Publishing.
6. Mike Donehey, "All Together," 2021, Musixmatch.

Questions for Reflection

1. When it comes to doubt, can you name times when you had to deal with it?

2. What are some areas in which you have had doubts: suffering, silence, speculation, or Scripture? What did you do about it?

3. Can you relate to Jacob's issue of not recognizing the presence of God in certain situations? Can you identify times like those in your life?

4. How comfortable are you with the idea that faith and doubt can coexist? Explain your thoughts.

5. When doubt bugs you, how do you normally respond to it? What do you do when you feel the darkness of doubt overwhelm you?

6. How can doubt strengthen your relationship with God? When you question God, and are honest with God, how does it make you feel?

CHAPTER EIGHT

UNANSWERED PRAYER AND GOD'S SILENCE

"I think I'm more familiar with fellowship that's fueled by coffee and donuts rather than prayer and fasting. Which means I might have a lot to learn about fellowship in the Spirit."
—Dave Rahn

I was on a call with some of my former students recently, and each of us shared some of the things we were doing. We always close with prayer requests.

All three of these individuals love God and love people. They are experts in their fields. They have all experienced adversity. I love each of them. They inspire me. They are fighters and have been quite resilient when it seemed God was quiet.

What is it that Annie, Lee, and LaToya have in common with you and me?

Prayers unanswered.

Annie's prayer for her marriage seemed to fail. LaToya's desire for marriage hasn't happened...at least not yet. Lee and his wife have prayed for a baby, but still no child...still waiting. Maybe you have heard the cliché, "God's timing is not our timing." That is sometimes an understatement.

Prayer is a powerful invitation to *meet* God. Prayer empowers us to have a relationship with God. Prayer is a big deal! It is not only our way to connect with Jesus, it is one of the ways Jesus connects with us. We also love and care for others when we pray.

As we pray, we are venturing into the world of unimaginable mystery and silence. It is a place of uncertainty, faith, doubt, surprises, and fascination that drive us to seek God. It opens the door to the ups and downs, the mountaintops and valleys of prayer.

We have all wrestled with unanswered prayer. And sometimes it feels like a book with blank pages.

Unanswered Prayers

In 1991, Dr. Jerry Sittser, an accomplished professor and historian, was in a catastrophic head-on vehicle collision with his family. In his book *Grace Disguised*, he writes about his struggle in the aftermath of that horrific experience:[1]

> I learned later that the alleged driver was Native American, drunk, driving eighty-five miles per hour. He was accompanied by his pregnant wife, who was killed in the accident. I remember those first moments after the accident as if everything was happening in slow motion.
>
> They are frozen into my memory with a terrible vividness. After recovering my breath, I turned around to survey the damage. The scene was chaotic...I saw the unconscious and broken bodies of Lynda, my four-year old daughter Diana Jane, and my mother. I remember getting Catherine (then eight), David (seven), and John (two) out of the van through my window, the only one that would open.
>
> I remember taking pulses, doing mouth-to-mouth resuscitation, trying to save the dying and calm the living. I remember the feeling of panic that struck my soul as I watched Lynda, my mother, and Diana Jane all die before my eyes. I remember the pandemonium that followed—people gawking, lights flashing from emergency vehicles, a helicopter whirring overhead, cars lining up, medical experts doing what they could do to help. And I remember the realization sweeping over me that I would soon plunge into a darkness from which I might never again emerge as a sane, normal, believing man...

---

1. Jerry L. Sittser, *A Grace Disguised: How The Soul Grows Through Loss* (Grand Rapids, Michigan: Zondervan, 2004), 26.

> Life was chaotic…responsibilities at home and work accumulated like trash on a vacant lot, threatening to push me toward collapse… I wondered whether I could survive another day, whether I wanted to survive another day. I felt punished by simply being alive and thought death would bring welcomed relief.

I read this story every semester in my counseling class, and I can barely get though it without some tears. I am a husband and father. I cannot imagine losing my wife, mom, and daughter in one fatal car wreck— gone in moments!

Like many of us feel at times, Dr. Sittser writes that he felt God had not answered his prayer:

> I prayed for my daughter's protection on the morning of the accident, as I had every morning since her birth. But something went terribly wrong that day. My prayer for Diana Jane was not answered, or so it seemed at the time.[2]

Chances are strong that you have prayed sometime in your life. And I'm going out on a limb here, but I'll bet you have asked God for something that came back with what you determined as a "no" to your request—or silence…no response.

God's Silence: A Model for Us?
Robert Cardinal Sarah was born in Guinea, West Africa. He was made an archbishop by Pope John Paul 11 and a Cardinal by Pope Benedict XVI.

He writes, "In my prayer and interior life, I have always felt the need for a deeper, more complete silence. I am talking about a kind of discretion that amounts to not even thinking about myself but, rather, turning my attention, my being, and my soul toward God."[3]

Sarah is raising the heart of the issue, where is our attention when we pray? Is it about *me or God?* My will or His? My being self-absorbed or God-focused?

---

2. Ibid., 37.
3. Robert Cardinal Sarah with Nicolas Diat, *The Power of Silence: Against the Dictatorship of Noise* (San Francisco: Ignatius Press, 2017), 21.

He continues, "The days of solitude, silence, and absolute fasting have been a great support. They have been an unprecedented grace, a slow purification, and a personal encounter with a God who wanted to draw me gradually toward a more substantial interior life so as to maintain an intimate relationship with him."[4]

My mentor in seminary, Gene Wilkins, used to tell our discipleship group, "The purpose of prayer is not getting an answer. The purpose of prayer is Him. That's it."

Solitude and silence are not an end in and of themselves; rather, they are a means to an end, and that end is encountering Jesus. We tend to think of prayer as a verbal list of requests. But Jesus tells us to not be like the Pharisees, who have many words (see Matthew 6:6–8).

Prayer's Paradigm

One of the great prayers mentioned in Holy Scripture was uttered by Samuel the prophet, when he was young: "Speak Lord for your servant is *listening*" (1 Sam. 3:9).

Could the paradigm shift be that *talking too much* during our prayer requests does not bring us that much closer to God? We hear God speak not so much when we are talking, but when we are listening.

Change the way you view prayer. Prayer is more listening than speaking. God speaks loudest when we are still.

Jesus and Silence

Jesus modeled *simplicity and silence*. The desert was his place of connection with His Father.

Matthew's Gospel takes us to a powerful scene—Jesus's baptism. It is a glorious moment. Jesus goes into the water and comes up: the "Spirit of God" was "descending like a dove alighting on him." (Matt. 3:16). Most of us who have been baptized have never had a dove alight on us following coming out of the water. We most certainly have not had the next experience: "And a **voice** from heaven said, 'This is my Son, whom I love; with him I am well pleased" (Matt. 3:17).

Blessings given from heaven with an audible voice. Powerful!

---

4. Ibid.

Following Jesus's baptism, He is *not* led into a parade or party with some Jerusalem wine. The Spirit of God, not the devil, leads Jesus to the wilderness (desert) to be tempted. And guess who is the tempter? None other than Satan himself (see Matthew 4:1).

It's a fairly normative pattern in Scripture: a victory is usually followed by a temptation. Jesus is under fire from the enemy. What does Jesus do during those forty days?

He *fasted* from food. And might I add, Jesus fasted from people sometimes. Jesus was in a solitary, lonely, deserted place. No Israeli hot spots, no spas or fancy restaurants. Just empty space. Wilderness. And snakes. Scorpions.

The wilderness is a place of *aloneness*, with the exception of some wild animals! Jesus follows the tradition of Abraham and Moses into the lonely world called the desert. It is a barren land. A place to be private. Wilderness is a place to learn and grow. It's not a vacation spot.

Jesus finds solitude and solace in the quiet places.

Jesus an Introvert?

If we follow the accounts of Jesus's life in the Gospels, we discover His model and pattern of prayer for us.

Matthew 14 records the narrative. Jesus hears that his friend and cousin, John the Baptist/baptizer, has been killed. What does Jesus do? "When Jesus heard what had happened, he *withdrew* by boat privately to a solitary place" (Matt. 14:13).

Jesus needed his "cave" time when he learned of John the Baptist's death. He escaped to be alone with His heavenly Father. But the crowds followed him, so he came out of hibernation and healed the sick (Matt. 14:14).

Later in the narrative of Matthew 14, Jesus performs a miracle we call the "feeding of the five thousand." So Jesus has been bombarded with 'people time" while he is stilling coping with the death of his cousin and friend.

Following the Matthew 14 scenario, we see Jesus making His "disciples get into the boat and go on ahead of him to the other side, while he dismissed the crowd" (Matt. 14:23). After He had dismissed them, he went up on a mountainside by himself to pray. Later that night, he was there alone" (Matt. 14:22–23).

Jesus sent his disciples out into a boat, and a storm emerged during the evening. Where was Jesus?

He was alone. By Himself. *Praying.*

Here's our model, folks! Sometimes we need to get away from the crowd, move away from the intensity of ministry and people, and go sit alone with God. I am not sure if we can argue one way or the other if Jesus was an introvert or extravert, and I'm not convinced it really matters.

Jesus certainly enjoyed people, loved to go to a wedding feast, enjoyed eating and feasting at people's homes, and spent three plus years constantly with his twelve disciples. Yet he was also ready to go off by Himself to pray. Jesus loved being alone with the Father to pray.

Does God Initiate?

We read in Scripture that God loves us and cares about us enough to listen to our prayers. And not only that, He *invites us to call on* His name. We read about it in the following passages: God hears our prayers, He is close to those who are brokenhearted, He comforts us in our afflictions, and He walks with us in the darkest valleys.

He is with us every step of the way: "The righteous cry out, and the Lord hears them; he delivers them from all their troubles. The Lord is close to the brokenhearted and saves those who are crushed in spirit" (Ps. 34:17–18). "Even though I walk through the darkest valley, I will fear no evil, for you are with me; your rod and your staff, they comfort me" (Ps. 23:4).

Prayer is an invitation to meet God. It is especially powerful when the answer comes back as "Yes." It's painful at times when God says, "Wait" or "No."

It Takes Two to Tango

Isaiah 40 declares that God will give strength to those who are tired and weak. We know that there are times He initiates with us, and there are times we initiate with Him. Prayer is a two-way street.

It is a dialogue, not a monologue.

Any relationship that is directed by only one individual is not a healthy, balanced relationship. A one-sided relationship is not a relationship. When one person who does all the initiation while the other person passively sits back, the two are not mutually engaged. It's the same with God—it takes two to tango. We do our part, God does His.

We may think of God as the primary initiator with humans, and sometimes that is accurate, but there are many accounts in which Jesus was not the initiator; rather, it was the person in pain coming to Jesus for help. Sometimes it was an individual rushing out to Jesus because of another person's affliction.

You Go Ninety

Does it matter who takes the first step in the relationship? In the movie *Hitch*, Will Smith plays Hitch, a matchmaking expert who is trying to teach Albert (Kevin James) about initiation in a dating relationship.

Hitch: "See, this is what most guys do. They rush in to take the kiss. But you're not most guys. See, the secret to a kiss is to go ninety percent of the way, and then hold."

Albert: "For how long?"

Hitch: "As long as it takes for her to come the other ten."

So who does the 90 percent in a relationship with God and humans? Who does the 10 percent? These are rhetorical questions because I don't think there is an exact science to how much God puts into it and the amount we put into it. We do see from Scripture some examples of who initiates, Jesus or people.

In Matthew chapters 8 and 9 are some examples of *people seeking* out Jesus first, not the other way around:

- "A man with *leprosy came and knelt before him* and said, 'Lord if you are willing, you can make me clean. Jesus reached out his hand and touched the man." (Matt. 8:2–3).
- "When Jesus had entered Capernaum, *a centurion came to him, asking* for *help*." (Matt. 8:5–6).
- 'When evening came, *many who were demon-possessed were brought to him*" (Matt. 8:16).
- *"Some men brought to him(Jesus)* a paralyzed man, lying on a mat" (Matt. 9:2).

In the narratives in Matthew chapters 8 and 9, the *person in need* reaches out to Jesus.

If He's not available to people, the action decreases. When Jesus is around, things happen!

In another passage, Jesus goes to Peter's home and notices that his mother-in-law is sick in bed with a fever, so He heals her (see Matthew 8:14–15).

No matter who initiates, when Jesus is in the vicinity, there is a connection.

Most venues described in these two chapters alone reveal that God *wants us to come to Him* with our hurts, pains, and needs.

Riskiness of Prayer for Healing

Prayer is risky. It can leave us disappointed when the answer that comes back is no, wait, or dead silence. Unanswered prayers are difficult to handle.

What happens if we ask and God does not heal or save or provide? Often, we have very specific needs that we believe God will answer and fulfill. And the two most unsettled areas for most people come in two categories: *healing* and *guidance*.

The lack of answered prayers for healing can be disheartening.

"Heal my son's_____." "Go before my friend, Scotty, who needs _____, or he will die."

The bottom line is that Scripture tells us to come before God with our requests. And in doing so, we have a stated agenda. With those strong feelings and needs, we get high hopes of God being able to deliver on what we see Him doing in the Bible.

News flash: We see Jesus healing people most of the time, *but not all the time.*

Some prayers will go unanswered in some shape or form.

We know that the writer of the Gospel of Luke was a doctor in his day. And Luke writes these words in Luke 7:21: "At that very time Jesus cured many who had diseases." It does not say "Jesus cured *all* who had diseases." Luke uses the word *many*, and in the Greek language, the implication is clear: not all were healed. I don't know why. It's a mystery as well on why God heals some but not others.

Some "prosperity gospel" individuals believe that if you are not healed, you lack faith. But that is insane because we all know godly men and women who believe that God can and *will* heal them, yet they don't experience the healing. This is the ultimate heartbreak for many.

We forget that God is the ultimate healer, and He also has human healers on Earth—doctors, nurses, physician assistants, front-line workers, surgeons, dentists, eye doctors, chiropractors, and many more people who care about our longevity and well-being.

I know some faith-oriented people who get mad when they have to go to a medical doctor. They presuppose that *only* God is the healer, and that if God does not do it supernaturally, then it must not be authentic.

Others believe God uses *only the medical world* to heal their pneumonia or cancer.

Some believe in miracles, others do not. Some trust doctors, some don't. Some trust God, others don't. It goes all directions.

Bottom line—if you get healed through any means, I think God should get the credit and the glory!

Unanswered Prayers for Guidance

The second place of discomfort is voicing prayers for *guidance* that seem unanswered. "Save my parents' marriage." "Where should I go to college?" "What should I do with my life?" "Do I get married to _____?"

Jesus actually uses an acrostic for praying—ASK. He tells us to ask, seek and knock (see Matthew 7:7). We do this often with guidance. When we feel like God is not listening, we get discouraged, and the temptation is to quit the ASK.

Desperate Measures

One insight to pay attention to in the Gospels is that all those who approach Jesus seem to be *desperate*.

And desperate people are in desperate situations living in desperate times. There are no other options than to *run* to Jesus.

Jairus is a synagogue elder. His daughter is dying. He throws himself at Jesus's feet and begs for mercy, asking Jesus to touch his sick daughter (see Mark 5). While Jesus is on the way with Jairus to heal the daughter, He is interrupted by a lady who has been hemorrhaging for twelve years and needs a cure. This woman, who was considered *unclean*, touches Jesus's garment because she believes He is the Messiah who heals people's diseases and afflictions. She is talking to herself, saying, "If only I can touch his clothes, I will become whole."

The woman risked everything. Embarrassment. Humiliation. The crowd was probably hissing and making noises because she touched a holy man. Jesus felt the touch and asked who it was. He then looked to her and said, "My daughter, your faith has made you well. Go in peace, and be healed of your trouble" (Mark 5:34, GNT).

Meanwhile, following the healing of the woman, Jesus heads to Jarius's house. When they arrive, the messengers tell Jesus that the twelve-year-old daughter has died. Jesus acts like he doesn't hear the bad news. He proceeds into the home and tells the girl to "get up." Jesus works another miracle.

People reaching out to Jesus. Each one, *desperate* for God.

Prayer Is Relational

Sometimes we reach out to God, and sometimes *God reaches out to us* without us asking anything.

In John's Gospel, there is an interesting flow of relationships:

- In John 2, Jesus is *invited* to a wedding in Cana and turns water into wine. The wedding *party initiated*, and Jesus responded to a need. The night was a huge success.
- In John 3, a leader of the Pharisees named Nicodemus approaches Jesus at night. Jesus responds to the conversation. *Human initiative.*
- In John 4, Jesus goes through the forbidden land of Samaria and does the initiation with a woman at the well, something that Jewish rabbis were not to do, especially with a woman and a Samaritan (half-breed). *Jesus initiates.*
- In John 5, Jesus asks the paralyzed man, "Do you want to get well?" and heals him. *Initiative by Jesus.*

Sometimes, people come to Jesus because of their need, and other times Jesus initiates the action because of their situation. There seems to be a balanced approach to prayer. One size does not fit all when it comes to prayer.

Following the wreck that took the lives of three family members, and that he and his remaining three children survived, Jerry Sittser writes the following:

> I realized in that moment that there was nothing I could do to reverse the catastrophe that had just devastated our family. But a few days later, a question arose in the back of my mind…Why are you praying, Jerry? You prayed for Diana Jane's protection the morning of the accident, and look what happened! Why didn't God answer that prayer? Can you take prayer seriously, ever again?[5]

Lessons to Ponder

When it comes to unanswered prayers, consider these four principles as we navigate these troublesome waters and the need to embrace the discipline of silence.

1. Rethink

Begin by rethinking issues about prayer and the nature of silence.

Is it possible that God does not answer some of our prayers because He knows we don't need the answer to always be *yes?* Just ask any parent… do we always say yes?

We focus sometimes on *what God didn't do.* Have you ever considered that there are some prayers God does not want to answer?

Have you ever looked back and thanked God for *not* answering some prayer? Maybe you dated a guy or girl and thought he or she would become your spouse, and you prayed for the relationship to work out, but it didn't. Well, God brought you someone better.

My college friend, Jonathan, who was on his way to becoming a great baseball player, injured his ACL. Even though Jonathan was bitter, angry, and depressed, he later realized that God allowed that situation to disrupt his dream of professional baseball. It turns out God wanted Jonathan to

5. Jerry Sittser, *When God Doesn't Answer Your Prayers: Insights to Keep You Praying with Greater Faith and Deeper Hope* (Grand Rapids, Michigan: Zondervan, 2003), 17–18.

be a youth pastor and church planter instead.

Take a moment to thank God for some unanswered prayers!

"Is unanswered prayer God's design to pull us into the unseen mystery of silence?

Rethink prayer.

2. Renounce

Can we stop expecting God to work like an iPhone or anything else that requires immediacy?

God is not on my time table. He is not on the clock, like the NFL draft day. He does not have to act immediately, even though we hate the pain of suffering and waiting.

What would it look like if God answered all our prayers with a yes? Would we ever learn anything? Would we ever learn to trust God? Would we ever be satisfied? Would we even need God? Probably not.

God is not a genie in a bottle.

When it comes to prayer, we don't get a two- to three-year detailed plan, do we? It is not a well-oiled machine, this thing called *prayer* or *intercession.*

A student come to my office the other day, wanting to discuss the direction of his life. He wanted me to foretell his future and God's will in fifteen minutes. Guess what? I couldn't. I told him to go pray about it!

Mystery.

Why won't God lay things out more simply? I think you know the answer—if God laid out the plan for us in a simple five-step process, we would never "ask, seek, and knock." We would not learn how to trust God. Learning to walk with God is exhilarating and frustrating. And disruptive.

In Genesis 12 1, God tells Abram to go on a journey: "The LORD had said to Abram, 'Leave your country, your people and your father's household and go to the land I will show you. I will make you into a great nation and I will bless you; I will make your name great, and you will be a blessing. I will bless those who bless you, and whoever curses you I will curse; and all peoples on earth will be blessed through you.'"

So Abram left Harran at the ripe age of seventy-five and took his wife, Sarai, and Lot, his brother's son, and headed to Canaan. Abram later became Abraham. All he knew was that God promised that he would be the father of a great nation: "By faith Abraham, when he was called, obeyed by going out to a place which he was to receive for an inheritance; and he went out, not knowing where he was going" (Hebr. 11:8, NAS).

Look at the phrase from Hebrews 11:9: "He went out, not knowing where he was going." Abram did not have a map or a compass. Just go, Abe. He did.

Where? He had *no idea* where he was going. That is the beautiful mystery of prayer. It is an unknown and often confusing journey. That's what makes prayer so powerful—the adventure and intrigue of the "What is next?" phase. Abram had no clue what was next.

The story line in Luke 18:1–8 illustrates a principle against immediacy. Jesus tells of a widow who has been unjustly wronged, and she goes before the judge. The judge's response is initially apathetic and indifferent. However, this woman has moxie, some chutzpah. She challenges the judge to hear her out. She pleads and nags and is relentless. She eventually wears him down.

Why did the judge give in? "…yet because this widow keeps bothering me, I will give her justice, so that she will not beat me down by her continual coming." (Luke 18:5, ESV).

Quick prayers are usually *shallow prayers*. Often, a twenty-second "God, I need… thank you" request has no real heart and soul to it; it's just fast. This widow kept approaching the judge with passion and persistence. She was driven for an answer.

Most people want prayer to be more like a map, a compass, something that makes sense out of what is really a mystery. The problem is, God does not give us a simple, laid-out blueprint. No master plan. No instantaneous answers all the time. It's a mystery that most of us hate.

Jesus is saying that because this woman kept knocking, seeking, asking—because of her tenacity, the judge gave in.

Renounce—God is not a slot machine.

3. Recall

One of my heroes is Joni Eareckson Tada.

On July 30, 1967, at the age of seventeen, Joni dove off the pier into the Chesapeake Bay and suffered a fracture between the fourth and fifth cervical levels. While in the hospital, she and her family would have to hear the tough news: she was paralyzed from the shoulders down. Joni would be a quadriplegic for the rest of her life, barring a miracle.

Joni prayed for that miracle—to be totally healed. She battled depression, anger, suicidal thoughts, and doubts. Who wouldn't, seriously? But God never healed her physically.

God *allowed* this injury to become something profoundly great for Joni and all the people she would influence. God takes broken pieces and turns them into marvelous pottery. We all have feet of clay. God can rebuild you and me into something beautiful and awesome.

Joni founded an organization years after her accident, Joni & Friends, that responds to the needs of those in the disability community. Joni became an inspiration to me way before we had our own special-needs son.

Joni sings, teaches, preaches, and draws pictures by holding a paintbrush between her teeth. She has written more than forty books, including *Joni*, which became a number-one international best seller. She also hosts summer camps for kids and adults with special needs. Chances are good that none of this would have happened for Joni had she not been a victim of that horrific accident one day in July 1967.

God used this situation for good. Joni serves God with a purpose.

I met her a few years ago when she spoke at the university where I teach. My secretary told me she saw Joni in a wheelchair on our campus, and I made a bolt to go see her. Joni was as humble a person as I've ever met. Kind, gracious, and compassionate. I said to her, "You are remarkable."

She asked, "Why?"

I told her that I travel around the country speaking to youth and college groups and often tell her story as an illustration of persistence and humility. I mentioned to Joni that if I had the same diving accident had happened to her, I would have probably caved in and turned to anger and bitterness.

Most would blow God off.

Joni told me, "Well, I was bitter for a while, but when I started praying for God to show me how good could come out of it, He opened the heavens to me."

Her ultimate healing will be at the resurrection, when she sees Jesus face to face and is free from her paralysis. Until then, she uses a wheelchair. Recall the life of Joni Eareckson Tada as an example for us all—God can take the worst situations and turn them into good for us and for others.

4. Remember

The grueling part of the Bible is that it *never* identifies *why* prayers are unanswered. We can look back and see why some prayers were answered yes, some no. You and I are still waiting to see the outcome of some prayers. Jesus said some things get resolved only through prayer and fasting.

When I don't know what to pray, the following are my go-to passages. They are a lifeline for me. Remember these verses when you get into a tough place emotionally and spiritually—when doubt, stress, and other hurdles raise their ugly heads:

> "Thy kingdom come, thy will be done…"
> —Matthew 6:10, NKJV

> "What He opens, no one can shut, what He shuts, no one can open."
> —Revelation 3:7

Pray regularly with these verses in mind, with open hands. It will help keep discouragement at bay. Pray for God's will when you are seeking guidance— "Thy kingdom come, thy will be done"—not my will. His will be done! When you want God to do something miraculous, pray that He will open a door that no one can close or close a door no one else can open. Ask God to do the opening or closing.

To me, these are not only the safest prayers; they are closest to the heart of God. These are the prayers that always keep us grounded.

As Jesus was preparing to face His own suffering and ultimately His death on the cross, He prayed this prayer:

> "Nevertheless, not my will, but yours, be done."
> —Luke 22:42

Jesus's prayer was answered—the will of God was being done for the salvation of the world. Praying "not my will, but yours, be done" is the *best* prayer. I have prayed for people's healing. Some got healed, and others did not. Some recovered, and some died. God *does not always answer yes.*

Our viewpoint is limited. Jerry Sittser says, "Unanswered prayer *according to our perspective* does not mean unanswered prayer according to God's. Likewise, unanswered prayer in the present moment does not mean unanswered prayer next month or next year or perhaps in the next century."[6]

Prayer is wonderful and bizarre and mysterious. And I think it's meant to be that way because God is bigger than us, and God's response to our prayers is never meant to be a simple formula. Relationships are meant to be dynamic, not static; it's the same with silence. And the same with prayers—even unanswered ones.

Big Takeaway: Don't let unanswered prayer keep you from talking and listening to God. Keep pounding, keep knocking, seeking, and asking. Keep listening. Rethink. Renounce. Recall. Remember.

Questions for Reflection

1. What have been some of the biggest unanswered prayers you have dealt with? How did you respond when these prayers went unanswered?
2. How does unanswered prayer affect you emotionally and relationally?
3. What are some ways to effectively deal with the disappointments of unanswered prayers?
4. Of the four strategies to deal with unanswered prayer, which of these four do you need right now—rethink, renounce, recall, and remember? Explain.

---

6. Ibid, 181–182.

CHAPTER NINE

CLOSE ENCOUNTERS OF THE THIRD KIND: FEAR, WORRY, AND ANXIETY

"Does not everything depend on our interpretation of the silence around us?"
—Lawrence Durrell

When I was ten years old, I went waterskiing for the first time with some friends. Because I was a rookie, I hesitated for hours before I had the courage to try it out. One of my friends went three times, another guy twice, and the others went at least once. By late afternoon, my buddies looked at me and said, "Olshine, man up. It's your turn."

For those who have never waterskied, here is what it's like. I jumped out of the boat into the water, and the driver of the boat gave me instructions on what to do next. He said, "Put your foot into the boot of the first ski, and when it is tight, slip the other one on."

This feat took me a while because I was doing all that while floating in the water, being held up by a small life jacket.

As the boat went around me in shark-like fashion, I put the left boot on, and I started to spin around in a circle. Then, as I tried to put the right ski on my foot, the left ski came off. I was in the water about thirty minutes before I got my act together. Finally, I raised my hand to signal that I was ready.

The boat began to pull me up. But there was a problem: they did not tell me to stand up. Funny, huh?

So the boat was pulling me, and I was in a baseball catcher's position.

I could see my friends motioning through the mist, as the waves were covering me: *"Get up! Get up!"* they were shouting. I stood up on my skis, and within seconds felt like I was on a bronco in a Texas rodeo, holding on for dear life.

Eventually, I relaxed.

I then noticed my friends pointing to my right. They began to scream, "Go over the wake!" I had no idea what they were talking about, but they kept pointing right, so I turned my skis in that direction, and lo and behold, I jumped the wake. I was doing great in my own mind, but I was getting tired. I weighed about 72 pounds sopping wet.

My friends forgot to tell me one very important detail: when you fall, *let go of the rope.*

Well, I leaned forward and began to fall into the water, but I didn't let go of the rope. It must have pulled me 100 yards or more, and when I finally let go, I realized two things—one, I lost my skis, and two: I lost my swim trunks.

My friends were cracking up. It was one of the most embarrassing moments of my life, and climbing back into the boat was pretty troubling for all. Even the fish turned away. It's pretty funny today when I tell the story, but in reality, it took me seven years to get the courage to ski again. When I did ski again at the age of seventeen I was able to keep my swim trunks on. You know how? Staple gun. Just teasing.

This example of my water-skiing adventure does reveal three powers at work in our lives every day: fear, worry, and anxiety. I was afraid to try to ski the first time, and then fear and worry kept me from trying again, for years.

Close Encounters

When it comes to distracting our inner life, there are three enemies that battle our soul almost daily. When you and I are wondering where God is working and cannot seem to find Him, chances are, fear, worry, and anxiety are lurking closely behind.

Fear, worry and anxiety are the close encounters of the third kind.

This three-headed alien attacks our hearts and minds and disrupts our lives. We begin to get more distracted. It's hard to concentrate. It's hard to pray, tough to listen.

Fear Not

I find it fascinating that the Bible tells us more than four hundred times to "fear not" or "be not afraid."

Why do you think God tells us that God has not given us a spirit of fear? Why does God tell us to be courageous and not afraid? "Have I not commanded you? Do not be afraid; and do not be discouraged" (Josh. 1:9).

Joshua was taking the baton of leadership from Moses and was the new leader of several million Israelites What a challenge before Joshua! Anyone involved in leading others know how scary it can be, and how lonely it can be, but leading millions would be crazy-frightening.

Why does God tell Joshua to "not be afraid?" *Because he was!*

Fear is real.

Why should we not fear? Here's the answer: "For the Lord your God is with you wherever you go" (Josh. 1:9, ESV). As God was with Moses, He is also with Joshua. And you and me.

We see another narrative with fear tucked away in Matthew 14. Jesus sends the disciples out onto the lake, knowing a storm would be coming. That was nice of Jesus, wasn't it? He stays on the mountain praying, while they battle strong winds and waves in the fishing boat.

In the wee hours between two and four in the morning, Jesus comes out toward the boat, walking on water, and the disciple Peter cries out to see who it is. They think it is a ghost. They think they are hallucinating. It's dark, scary, and raining outside.

Peter says, "Lord if it's you, then tell me to come, and I will." (This is comical. Who *else* could it be?)

Jesus says "Come."

Peter jumps out of the boat while the other eleven disciples watch and giggle. Peter starts to walk on water. But he takes his eyes off Jesus and gazes at the wind, storm, and waves, so he begins to sink. He screams to Jesus, "Save me, Lord!" and Jesus throws Peter back into the boat.

Peter was brave and courageous.

The disciples make fun of him because he started to sink, yet he was the only one to jump out of the boat! We always make a joke out of Peter, but guess who didn't get out of the boat? The other disciples, who were taught, as "students," to do whatever the Rabbi did.

Peter actually had the *chutzpa* to walk on water—not on a calm night, but during a fierce storm. The other eleven stayed in the boat. Why did they not get out and follow their Rabbi, their Messiah? I'm putting my money on the main reason they were stuck in the boat: *fear*. Peter became afraid while he walked on water, but the other eleven stayed in the boat because of fear.

Fear *distracts*. When Peter saw the storm, and focused on the fear of what could happen and the possibility of him sinking, he lost sight of Jesus.

Fear *unnerves us*. Peter was lost in his ability to stay locked into Jesus in the midst of the violent storm. Most of us can relate. We get a bad medical report, and we become fixated on the negative rather than the possibilities.

Fears make us *restless*. I admire Peter. At least out of the twelve disciples, one was willing to take the plunge out of the boat. I mean, there had never been a Walking on Water 101 class, to my knowledge. This was a "new normal" for Peter. No Old Testament prophets had walked on water; Jesus appears to be the first. Because this was a new adventure, Peter was nervous, excited, impulsive, and restless. Peter wonders, "What if this does not go well? What if I drown?"

Fear battles within our minds. It makes solitude and quiet reflection nearly impossible at times. What can you do with the fears that wrap around your heart and brain? Fear unravels our emotions and makes it hard to focus on Jesus—storm or no storm.

Worry Turns Our Focus Away From God

Worry is the next troublemaker to divert our minds off God. Worry is a brain game. To *worry* means to have a "divided mind." Worry resides in our heads, in our thought process. It is mental, but it is also emotional and spiritual. Worry focuses on specific events and is triggered by situations and our reactions.

The classic case study is Luke 10:38–42. In this brief passage, we meet two sisters, Mary and Martha. They invite Jesus over for some lox and bagels. Martha is a *tasker*. She is also a worrywart as she prepares the meal for her Messiah. She could get the MVP award for worrying. Martha's a *doer*. She loves getting things done around the pad. John 11:5 tells us that Jesus loves Mary and Martha. He knows them well: "Martha was *distracted* by all the preparations that had to be made" (Luke 10:40).

Martha was concerned that her sister, Mary, was doing *nothing* around the house. Martha might be a firstborn, classic type A personality, driven by perfectionism, and who wouldn't want the house immaculate, knowing Jesus is coming for dinner? Somebody's got to prepare and cook the meal, right?

What is sister Mary doing while Martha is cleaning the crib? She is sitting at the feet of Jesus, listening to His words. While Martha is working, Mary is worshipping. And if you asked Mary and Martha, both might say what they were *doing* was worship.

Worry is specific. It is directly connected to something that impacts us. Martha says, "Lord, don't you care that my sister has left me to do the work by myself? Tell her to help" (Luke 10:40).

Pity party by Martha. "Lord, don't *You* care?" (We ask the same question to Jesus sometimes, too!).

How does Jesus react? "Martha, Martha, you are *worried and upset about many things*" (Luke 10:41).

"Martha, Martha" is a term of endearment.

Jesus does not correct Martha for working hard, but He does rebuke her about worrying too much. He gives her the solution: silence over service. Jesus praises Mary's act of quiet devotion.

Mary chooses silence, sitting before Jesus. We would call Mary a "contemplative" in today's world, one who is content with silence over noise: "Few things are needed—or indeed only one. Mary has chosen what is better, and it will not be taken away from her" (Luke 10:42).

Worry or worship? Which is the best option? Jesus says it's worship. Worship tames worry.

Worship Replaces Worry

During Jesus's times of preaching, His longest message is called the Sermon on the Mount, recorded in Matthew chapters 5–7. Jesus talks about vows, marriage, divorce, prayer, fasting, treasures, judging others, anger, adultery, and loving our enemies.

Of all the subjects He covers in those three chapters, the one He gives most attention to is that of *worry*. That's right, worry. Matthew 6:24–

35 is an extensive teaching by Jesus on worry, which means it's a pretty universal problem to address and solve.

I want to point out a few key words to help you understand where worry comes from and what to do about worry. If we can get a handle on worry, we can learn to settle into a better rhythm of listening to Jesus's voice.

Everything hinges on one word: *devoted*.

Jesus begins with comparing loving money or God and says we cannot do one without hating the other. He then transitions into a list of "do not worry" rebukes: don't worry about life, food, shelter, and clothing. He tells his listeners that the Father feeds the birds and takes care of them, and how much more will God make sure we are provided for? We are more valuable than birds. And more valuable than the flowers of the field (see Matthew 6:26).

Devotion Reveals Worry

Rabbi Jesus is the master at *asking questions*. Sometimes, He asked so many questions that His disciples were afraid to answer. They worried that they either wouldn't know the answer or might get reprimanded for giving the wrong answer.

Some of his questions were rhetorical: "Are you more important than the birds? Are you more valuable than the flowers?"

Yes and yes are the right answers to Jesus. Good job. Congrats. A-plus grade: "Either you will hate the one and love the other, or you will be *devoted* to the one and despise the other" (Matt. 6:24).

In essence, Jesus is asking us, "What are you *devoted* to?" Our answer to that question will reveal what we are most concerned about, what we *worry* about. The things we are *devoted to are the trigger points to our deepest worries.*

Devotion reveals what causes us to worry. Some of my youth-group and college students worry about their grades. They worry about having a high GPA because some of them want to go on for more education. Grades matter to them.

When I lay my head down on the pillow at night, I do not lose one minute of sleep over their grades. Do you know why I don't lose sleep over whether they get and A or B? Is it that I do not care? Nope, I care.

What is the real reason I don't have insomnia when it comes to their GPAs? I am not *devoted* to their grades!

My neighbor is facing some financial choices. I am concerned. I pray for him, but I do not worry about his 401(k) account. Why? I am *not devoted* to his retirement plan. The areas of life that we are most devoted to make us most vulnerable to worrying.

Jesus says the flowers of the field *do not spin* or labor.

I used to think that people don't sleep well because they don't go to bed early enough or aren't taking enough melatonin, when in reality, they are tossing and turning in bed because they are worried. They are spinning out of control with worry. The things we are *devoted* to are those issues that we worry about the most.

What is in your spin cycle—what are you worrying about these days?

Jesus tells us at least four times, "Do not worry," which used to bug me. It's like when you are little and your parents tell you, "Go to sleep," but you can't. Could it be that Jesus has a reason for us to "not to worry"?

Jesus asks the question, "Can any one of you by worrying add a single hour to your life? (Matt. 6:27). Jesus is asking a profound question—can worry add *more hours* to your life? The answer is an obvious *no*. A reflective question is hidden in the original question—can worry *take* hours off your life? Yes!

He is saying that worry will steal time from our lives. Worry is destructive to our ability to learn to be quiet and listen to God. Worry will send our minds somewhere that is unproductive for our souls. My wife says worry is "filling up your time and space long before you get there."

From Worry to Worthy

What's the solution?

Jesus said in Luke 10 that Mary's choice of sitting at his feet would not only be the highest priority, but that he would *never take it away.* In Matthew 6:33, He reiterates what he told Martha about Mary in a different setting, but with a similar framework: *"Seek first his kingdom and his righteousness, and all these things will be given to you as well"* (Matt. 6:33).

The Kingdom of God does not refer to heaven; it speaks of the "rule and reign of God." Seek first, above all else, the Lordship of Jesus, not second, third, fortieth, or one-hundredth. Put God first. Worship will help reduce worry. That is why sitting in silence is so huge, because we can then center all our worries and thoughts and offer them to God.

We are then able to turn our *worry into something worthy*—the Kingdom. Then we can truly rest.

Anxiety

Worry and anxiety are close cousins, but very different. Both are equally powerful and are good at dismantling our time with God. Anxiety is a great distractor. Anxiety is often more generalized than worry. *Worry* tends to plague our minds, whereas *anxiety* affects our minds and bodies. Some foods, such as coffee and chocolate, can stimulate anxiety in us and cause a physical reaction. I have approached a number of speaking engagements after drinking too much coffee, and it added to my anxiety about the presentation. It caused me to feel faint and nauseated and to have low blood sugar.

What is anxiety? Here's my definition: *Anxiety is worry on steroids.*

Worry and fear create anxiety. Most of the time, worry is short term and abbreviated. Anxiety can be painstakingly long and feels like forever. Anxiety can invade our minds and emotions, which impacts our daily living. Some teens and adults are diagnosed with anxiety disorders and need medication to keep them functioning at a normal cadence and equilibrium.

Anxiety can be triggered by our own fears and beliefs. It can also be a pattern from our family systems. Anxiety is often a result of a fear or dread of a past or upcoming event. *Anticipatory anxiety* is when you think you will have a recurring event happen again.

Let's say you get sick on a Friday night. Then, as the following Friday approaches, you may fear and get anxious that the sickness is coming on again. That is a hard to live with, and some people experience this on a regular basis.

Anxiety is mentioned in 1 Peter 5:7 in the context of humbling ourselves, praying, and resting in God. Peter was a fisherman before he started following Jesus. He continued to fish on occasion. He uses fisherman language: *"Cast* all your *anxiety* on him..."* Like a fishing net, we cast our anxieties into the sea of God's care.

Why? Because…"He cares for you."

Anxiety attacks us. It's real. An enemy.

"Anxiety weighs down the heart, but a kind word cheers it up" (Prov. 12:25).

That is a great word picture of anxiety, isn't it? Anxiety *weighs* the heart down. Anxiety and the effects it has on us are heavy on our physical hearts.

My friend, Dr. Steve Johnson, is a psychotherapist. He lists some of the symptoms of anxiety:

- Avoidance of certain places and people
- Difficulty concentrating
- Dry mouth
- Excessive worry
- Feeling on edge
- Insomnia
- Irritation
- Rapid pulse
- Restlessness
- Sweaty palms
- Uncomfortable urge to move

I find it really hard to get still before God when my brain is full of worry, anxiety, and fear. It's tough to be quiet and silent when we are doing mind warfare, isn't it?

Three Strategies for Overcoming Worry, Anxiety, and Fear

What can we do with these three close encounters as they relate to entering God's world of silence and making the most of our time resting in Him? Here are three key principles: Leave, decompress, and ask. Let's explore each strategy.

1. Leave

As you take your concerns to Jesus, learn to leave them with him. I carry around a backpack, and sometimes it gets heavy. Imagine if I placed heavy rocks in it, and each one of them had a name:

- Worries about finances
- Fears of failure
- Anxieties about my future
- Fears of losing my wife or kids
- Health issues

All those heavy burdens inside my backpack are starting to weigh me down. I must learn to take each item out of the backpack and place it before Jesus. I need to name each one of them and let them go: "I *sought* the Lord, and He answered me. He delivered me from all my fears" (Ps. 34:4).

We were never intended to carry these around all day. Release. You and I can learn to rely on God to ease our fears, worries, and anxieties. Leave them at the cross of Jesus: "When I am afraid, I put my *trust in you*" (Ps. 56:3).

2. Decompress

Paul the apostle writes of the warfare and battle for our minds in 2 Corinthians 10:5. He tells us, "The weapons we fight with are not the weapons of the world. On the contrary, they have divine power to demolish strongholds. We demolish arguments and every pretension that sets itself up against the knowledge of God, and we take captive every thought to make it obedient to Christ."

Paul is making it crystal clear that there is a spiritual warfare going on. Where is the battlefield? In our minds. Wars begin there. Paul tells us to take these thoughts "captive" and give them to Christ Jesus. Every thought.

We have been given divine power to decompress from worry, fear, and anxiety.

These three enemies are considered "strongholds," which means they can grab our minds and emotions and hold us in bondage. Some of these thoughts are telling us the worst-case scenarios about our lives, and some of them are lies from Satan about us and God. They come into our heads as "arguments" and "pretensions" that go against God. That's probably why sometimes some of the internal "still, small voices" we might hear are not from the Holy Spirit, but rather are from the accuser, the devil, speaking words of deception to us. He plants these kinds of ideas into our heads: "God does not care about you." "You are all alone." "You have nothing to live for."

Give all your thoughts to Jesus. Don't carry them around. Let them go. Jesus told the storm to be silent! Decompress with some silence.

3. Ask

Clay Christensen, a professor at Harvard Business School, said, "Questions are places in your mind where answers fit. If you haven't asked the question, the answer has nowhere to go. It hits your mind and bounces right off. You have to ask the question—you have to want to know—in order to open up for the space for the answer to fit."[1]

That is an excellent perspective. What questions do you need to ask that are related to fear, worry, and those things that make you anxious? Here are a few to get you started. Ask God for some answers:

- God, why am I worried?
- God, what does fear do to me when I am trying to be still and pray?
- Lord, how does anxiety break up my silence?
- What steps can I take to surrender these concerns to You, God?

As you learn how to leave your burdens to God and decompress, ask *God for courage.* That was the remedy, the antidote for fear with Moses and Joshua, and it will aid you in solving your worry and anxieties issues as well. Remember the promise of God to help Joshua overcome fear and discouragement? It was rooted in these four powerful words:

Be strong and courageous.

Ask God for strength and courage, and you will notice that you are beginning to be more comfortable with the idea of mystery and silence. You will emerge with a new story to write about your life.

In the 2013 movie *The Secret Life of Walter Mitty*, Walter, played by

---

1. Andy Stanley, *Better Decisions, Fewer Regrets* (Grand Rapids, Michigan: Zondervan, 2020), .3

Ben Stiller, is a dreamer who typically "zones out" imagining himself doing great things. However, he is impotent as it relates to courage and action. His colleague, Sheryl Melhoff (played by Kristen Wiig) says to Walter, "Life is about courage and going into the unknown."

She is right, you know. As you start making better decisions about the right things to be devoted to, you will start helping others embrace the mystery of silence as well. Learn to let go of worry. Fear. Anxieties.

Start writing or rewriting your story today; it matters to God and others.

Have courage to step into the great unknown.

Big Takeaway: When it comes to the three-headed monster of fear, worry, and anxiety, learn to follow the three-step pattern for gaining some victory: leave, decompress, and ask.

Questions for Reflection
1. How do you reconcile faith with fear, worry, and anxiety?
2. Regarding the three-headed monster of fear, worry and anxiety, which of the three burdens raises its up ugly head at you the most?
3. What do fear, worry, and anxiety do to you when you are trying to embrace times of silence? How do you handle the interruptions and disruptions?
4. What are some ways worry keeps your emotions bottled up?

CHAPTER TEN

HURT AND GRIEF: JOB'S CATACLYSMIC EXPERIENCE

"King Peppy: It's a story as old as time. In the beginning, there was silence."
—Trolls World Tour

Hurt and grief. These feelings come naturally if you ever find yourself being a parent. Our kids will give us unspeakable joy, and they can also break our hearts.

Tears are often a result when we face hurt and grief. I am not big-time crier, but I have cried a number of times in my life. I've cried over losing my dogs. I've cried at weddings and funerals. I cried at my own wedding. I teared up at the birth of both my children. I've cried over *Hallmark* commercials. Tears are good.

I cried a lot in Andrew's first forty days. I had the honor and joy of speaking at my daughter's high-school graduation and cried during my commencement talk. It was such a good talk, even I wanted to take notes on it! I cried at my daughter's wedding. I cried at her baby shower. I cry at ESPN documentaries. You get my jam.

One of the scariest and tearful moments happened when Andrew turned sixteen. He and I were going to play in a national Special Olympics tennis doubles match in Hilton Head, South Carolina. On the afternoon before the tournament match, Andrew was taking a bath in our hotel room, and Rhonda noticed dark spots all over his body. We were concerned and called our pediatrician, who suggested that we go to urgent care. We did.

The doctors took a blood test and said his platelets were extremely low. They sent us to the emergency room at the hospital, and the doctor there also did a blood test. The ER doc said we needed to get back to our hometown immediately, and he arranged for an ambulance to take Andrew and Rhonda back to Columbia, South Carolina. The doctor mentioned the possibility of leukemia. I freaked out.

Rhonda and Andrew took the ambulance back home, and I headed back to the condo to get all our clothes, pack up the car, and head to Children's Hospital. By that time, it was about 11:00 p.m., pitch black outside, and I got lost driving back to the condo in Hilton Head.

I began to wail and weep, not just because I was lost (and directionally challenged); I was also thinking the worst. My tears were full of fear and sadness and anger and grief and pain. I was shouting out to God, "You cannot let my boy die! He is too young. You cannot have him yet! We have waited too long to watch him grow up. Spare his life, God!"

When I finally arrived at the condo, the night security guy helped me pack up the van. I thanked him and made the three-hour trek back home. I cried most of the way, and then God somehow gave me a feeling of peace. Meanwhile, Rhonda was in the ambulance, praying the entire time. They arrived at the hospital about 2:30 am and I got there about 3:15 am.

We settled in at the hospital and all stayed in Andrew's room. The doctors and nurses were phenomenal. We ended up being there two nights, and they gave Andrew some plasma plus medicine to tell the body's blood platelets to stop attacking his system. The doctor outsmarted Andrew's platelets. There was never a diagnosis of leukemia. That was one scary event as parents. We could have filled up a bottle of tears. We left the hospital relieved for the outcome, that Andrew's system was getting back to normal.

Tears Are Therapy

Hurt and grief make it really difficult to listen to the whisper.

In fact, we go from the *ability hear from God to the inability* to hear from God because hurt and grief become huge defense mechanisms. When we are emotionally distraught and broken, the last thing on our minds is hearing from God. It's nearly impossible to be silent until we manage our emotions in a healthy manner. Sometimes, we need to call a time-out to settle down. Before that can happen, we just need to let it out. Tears can be therapeutic.

We humans don't handle hurt and grief very well. People of faith don't always grieve well, as a matter of fact. I struggle big time in this area because when pain and suffering come into my life, and I feel hurt and start the grieving process, my mind and emotions are all over the place. I am distracted and have trouble concentrating. I will start reading a Bible passage and check out seconds later. Can I get a witness?

C. S. Lewis lost his wife to cancer and writes this about grief: "No one ever told me that grief felt so much like fear. I am not afraid, but the sensation is like being afraid. The same fluttering in the stomach, the same restlessness, the yawning. I keep on swallowing. At other times it feels like being mildly drunk, or concussed. There is a sort of invisible blanket between the world and me. I find it hard to take in what anyone says. Or perhaps, hard to want to take it in. It is so uninteresting. Yet I want the others to be about me. I dread the moments when the house is empty. If only they would talk to one another and not me."[1]

Dr. Elie Wiesel also knew grief. Wiesel, who survived Auschwitz, wrote, "My tradition teaches that no heart is as whole as a broken heart, and I would say that no faith is as solid as a wounded faith."[2]

Our souls are vulnerable. So when (not *if*) someone hurts us, we become disillusioned and disappointed. We might get angry and aggressive. We might try to bury the hurt and pain. This leads to discouragement or even depression. Hurt and grief become two of the biggest distractors and detractors when it comes to learning to be silent and hearing the voice of God.

Case Study: Job

The Bible isn't shy when it comes to talking about people in pain. That's one of the reasons I love the Scriptures. One character from the Bible who had devastating experiences was the man named Job (not *job*, as in work). Some scholars believe Job is the oldest of the Old Testament books. He was a great guy, a man of outstanding character and integrity.

---

1. C. S. Lewis, *A Grief Observed* (New York: HarperOne, 1961), 3.
2. Dominic Done, *When Faith Fails*, 154.

163

He was well liked and wealthy. Job had plenty of property, animals, and a wife and kids. Job was godly.

Listen to chapter one's account of Job: "There was a man in the land of Uz whose name was Job, and that man was blameless and upright, one who feared God and turned away from evil. There were born to him seven sons and three daughters" (Job 1:1–2, ESV).

Job is the Jeff Bezos (aka Amazon.com) of the Bible. He had everything—a home, property, lots of land, seven thousand sheep, three thousand camels, five hundred oxen, five hundred female donkeys. Great servants. A wife and children. Life was good, and God was good—that is, until it was all taken away. Life came crashing down on Job.

Satan, the accuser, went to God in the heavenly courts and challenged God to afflict Job: "The Lord said to Satan, 'From where have you come?' Satan answered the Lord and said, 'From going to and fro on the earth, and from walking up and down on it.' And the Lord said to Satan, 'Have you considered my servant Job, that there is none like him on the earth, a blameless and upright man, who fears God and turns away from evil?' Then Satan answered the Lord and said, 'Does Job fear God for no reason?'" (Job 1:7–9).

God allowed Satan to test Job.

The narrative continues: "Have you not put a hedge around him and his house and all that he has, on every side? You have blessed the work of his hands, and his possessions have increased in the land. But stretch out your hand and touch all that he has, and he will curse you to your face.' And the Lord said to Satan, 'Behold, all that he has is in your hand. Only against him do not stretch out your hand.' So Satan went out from the presence of the Lord" (Job 1:7–12, ESV).

Destruction entered the world of Job and his family.

Raiders came in and ravaged his place. They stole all the animals and murdered the servants. Lightning struck the sheep, and Job's children were killed by a tornado. Talk about a nightmare that could only be scripted in a Hollywood movie—and that was just day one.

Job lost everything. This book is about suffering, but it's more about how we respond to difficulty. God was trying to speak to Job, yet Job was so throttled by his losses that he had trouble concentrating on anything other than his pain.

His kids—seven boys and three girls—were gone. Dead. Job was beside himself and did the ancient custom of tearing his robe, shaving his hair, and worshipping God. He prayed the unthinkable: "The Lord gave and the Lord has taken away. Blessed be the name of the Lord" (Job 1:21).

Satan went back to God again…the adversary wanted to create more misery for Job. Satan implanted boils from the bottom of Job's feet to the top of his head, and he was in such anguish that he used broken pottery to scrape the boils. He was tormented day and night.

Job was in emotional and physical distress. It's mind-boggling to think of Job's loss—and Satan was loving it. Too late to call State Farm for an estimate. Job sank in misery—and who wouldn't have?

Job's wife insisted that he "curse God and die." Basically, Mrs. Job believed death would be better than a lifetime of grief and hurt.

Likewise, some people feel that suicide is an enticing option.

The husband of our friend, Sugar Kyzer Jeffcoat, took his own life. She said in a podcast, "Suicide is an act of selfishness. C. J. suffered for years with post-traumatic stress syndrome and chose to ignore it most of the time. Just remember, if you're ever thinking about harming yourself, just know those people, who you think will forget about you—*they do not.* Suicide doesn't stop the pain; it only *shifts* it."

The pain for some is deep and dark.

How much pain can a human put up with? How many hits to the gut can a person take in a day? Job had four, and they were catastrophic! Two natural disasters (winds and fire) and then two different invading troops. Job ended up with nothing—bankrupt and childless. The grief was out of control for Job.

Now, remember this: Job did not know about "the book of Job" or the outcome of the story!

How did Job handle adversity and God's subtle silence?

Job believed that God *allows* both heartache and blessings. How do we know that? Job says it to his wife. Sometimes it's hard for men to convince their wives of things! Job said it straight in 2:9–10: "Shall we indeed accept good from God and *not accept* adversity? In all of this Job did not sin with his lips" (Job 2:10).

Sitting Shiva

The story of Job continues to unfold. He has three friends who see Job in his affliction. They give us a template to work with when it comes to being helpful—and the opposite: ways to not inflict more pain on those who are suffering. We observe what to do and what *not do* when it comes to *counseling* others.

They approach Job, which is good. They *initiate* the relationship and see him in great suffering. The most powerful thing they do for Job, initially, is to keep their mouths shut. For seven days, they sat with Job and grieved with him.

The rabbis call this "sitting Shiva." It refers to the act of sitting either on the ground or on low stools and mourning with the person in agony. Job's friends teach us a powerful lesson on what to do when another human being is suffering: Grieve with those who grieve. Listen well. Sit in silence. Be fully present.

For seven days and nights, Job's friends sat and mourned with him. And they said *not one word.* That is pretty impressive. Most of us cannot be quiet for seven minutes.

But as you know, all good things come to an end, and Job's friends—Eliphaz, Bildad, and Zophar—could not help themselves any longer. They felt they must voice their ideas and opinions! When they did, the conversation went from bad to worse.

Words can get us into trouble.

The three "stooges" said, basically, "Hey, Job, all this calamity has come onto you because your kids were partying and sinned; plus, you were a lousy father. You let them do whatever they wanted. And by the way, you are sinful, too, and God sent His judgment on you."

Ouch! Nice friends, huh? As the narrative continues, Job has some things to say: "After this Job opened his mouth and *cursed* the day of his birth" (Job 3:1). He was in such anguish that he wished he had never been born.

He then illustrates how he really feels as a grieving parent: "For the thing that I fear comes upon me, and what I dread befalls me. I am not at ease, nor am I quiet; I have no rest, but trouble comes" (Job 3:25–26, ESV).

Job was not a happy camper.

I cannot imagine losing everything in one day, can you? Family, fortune, and fame.

Grieved Out

Job started on a rant, and I think this is a great message for all of us. When in pain, be honest with God. As I mentioned, we should tell God when we struggle with doubts. We should also be ruthlessly transparent with God over our hurt and grief. Job had so many questions—the main two were, "Why is God silent?" during horrific experiences like his own, and "Why me?"

This isn't just the story of Job; it's also the story about us and our lives and questions: "Therefore I will not restrain my mouth; I will speak in the anguish of my spirit; I will complain in the bitterness of my soul" (Job 7: 11, ESV).

Job needed to vent about God's seeming absence from this tragedy: "I cry to you for help and you do not answer me; I stand, and you only look at me. You have turned cruel to me; with the might of your hand you persecute me. You lift me up on the wind; you make me ride on it, and you toss me about in the roar of the storm. For I know that you will bring me to death and to the house appointed for all living" (Job 30:20–23, ESV).

Job was seething for many reasons.

First, he was in tremendous suffering over the significant loss of his kids, property, and wealth. Who wouldn't be? Second, he and his wife were on different pages. Mrs. Job was angry and bitter, while Job was in a relational triangle and torn between her feelings about life and God. He wanted to think right, believe right, and act right about the circumstances. When a person is in the midst of emotional turbulence, it's easy to be theologically and mentally illogical. Third, he was tired of the rhetoric and bad theology of his three friends. Fourth, his pain seemed unresolvable. And finally, Job knew that God is God. Job believed he did not deserve this "punishment." Job thought he had done nothing wrong, yet he had nothing to really stand on.

Disastrous Loss

Jerry Sittser explains the jolt of a catastrophe: "Cataclysmic loss by definition precludes recovery. It will transform us or destroy us, but it will never leave us the same. There is no going back to the past…It is not therefore true that we become less through loss—unless we allow the loss to make us less, grinding our soul down until there is nothing left… Loss can also make us more. I did not get over the loss of my loved ones; rather, I absorbed the loss into my life…until it became part of who I am. Sorrow took up permanent residence in my soul and enlarged it…One learns the pain of others by suffering one's own pain, by turning inside oneself, by finding one's own soul…However painful, sorrow is good for the soul…the soul is elastic, like a balloon. It can grow larger through suffering."[3]

Job was hurting, which made it hard for him to sense the hand of God.

Had Job *left* his faith? Hardly.

Had Job *lost* his faith? He did not. Job was actually explaining, expressing, and examining his own faith. He was wrestling and thrashing with God.

How did God respond to Job?

God *never* answered Job's questions with linear responses. He did, however, respond with *questions* that were directly related to creation.

Time for Some Closure

The Book of Job contains forty-one chapters. It's a long book. Nine of these chapters are speeches from Job's three friends. At the end of the book, God says the guys have *misrepresented* Him; they have spoken incorrectly about God's plans and nature. God did not appreciate their poor theological views and said they needed to change their tune and apologize to Job for what they said to him.

In chapters 38 and 39, God asks Job a set of serious rhetorical questions. I will summarize these for clarity:

- Where were you when I created the Earth?
- Who decided on the size of the planet?
- Who came up with the measurements and blueprints?

Why do we both love and despise the book of Job? We love the book of

---

3. Jerry Sittser, *A Grace Disguised*, 37, 39, 44, 61.

Job because his story is like *our* stories. We all have suffered in life. We all have had losses. We all have had pain. We like the book for those reasons.

We dislike the book because the problems of suffering and tragedies are not given a simple theological answer. However, as much as it hurts us to not have an easy resolution to the problems of evil, we can *love* the book of Job because it *doesn't* give a clear way to understand the issues of loss and sorrow. It normalizes our pain.

We like the ambiguity because we know we have had the same question of "Why?" when it comes to our own stories. This is both comforting and troubling. We relate in some ways to Job's loss. We connect in many ways to unanswered questions and mystery. God does not chart out elementary answers. He does go back, however, to questions about His creation: "Who took charge of the ocean? Who do you know that can create light from darkness? Did you create the horses to prance and dance? What do you know about the hawk's ability to fly? Did you teach the eagle how to fly?"

What do these questions from God to Job mean? And what do they mean for us? God was telling Job, basically, these concepts in an intuitive way: "I made the world. I made you. You don't have to have everything figured out all the time. You don't need to know the 'why' to everything. You have a choice—will you trust Me in the midst of all the ache, hurt, and confusion? Or will you try to rely on your own intelligence?"

In the last chapter, Job finally admits that he should have not talked too much, that he misspoke at times, and that he should have listened (Job 40:4). There's that theme again—listening. Job is silent.

Next Steps: The ABCD Approach

What do we need to do when we want to hear God's voice, but we're in the midst of hurt and grief? How do we work through it and still keep an open heart, with eyes to see and ears to hear?

I like to teach my college students about the ABCD approach to working through this process of suffering. The "A" is to *acknowledge* the various stages of grief and loss.

A: Acknowledge the cycle of grief.

Elizabeth Kubler-Ross made famous the stages of handling grief. Grief is a natural response to the loss of anything, whether it is a loved one, innocence, a favorite pet, a relationship, a job, a marriage, or a dream.

• **Stage 1—Denial.** This is when we refuse to accept the tragedy and loss. We had ongoing bouts of grief with our son, Andrew. The thickest season of grief was the first forty days. It subsided for a while and then raised its head again and again. There was a season when we could not believe that God would allow us to have a child with Down syndrome. And then we became more comfortable with it as the days marched onward.

Denial means you have a hard time believing that "what happened" actually *did* happen. A season of shock. Times of feeling stunned. A dear friend of ours from our graduate-school days lost her husband recently to a heart attack. One minute, he was working around the house, and then he dropped to his knees and was gone. Abby said she could not believe it and could "barely breathe." Unexpected death or any loss leads to denial, and denial takes the wind out of us.

• **Stage 2—Anger.** This is frustration over the unfairness of an event. Anger usually emerges because the person does not understand why the event happened and because of severity of the experience feels unjust and unfair. That leads to a feeling of anger.

• **Stage 3—Bargaining.** This is when the sufferer attempts to "make a deal" to lessen the pain. Let's say you just learned that you lost your job, primarily because you were continually late. Bargaining would be where you start praying, "God, I will never be late again if you could just give me one more chance." At this stage, fear and anxiety emerge, add in some, guilt and feelings of helplessness.

• **Stage 4—Depression.** Sadness begins to settle in. These can be depressing and gloomy days for sufferers. They may experience physical effects like tightness in the throat, feeling exhausted, or losing their appetite. There is a deep pit of aloneness and heaviness of the soul, with some doubt and sorrow. A sense of hopelessness emerges in this stage.

• **Stage 5—Acceptance.** In this last stage, the person who is suffering begins to see some light at the end of the tunnel. The one who is experiencing pain and suffering begins the hard work of recovery through new insights and understanding.

May I add one more to the list?

• **Stage 6—Hope.** The person experiencing hurt and grief starts to embrace some of the loss. He or she starts to embrace the situation and moves forward. "Hope deferred makes the heart sick, but a dream fulfilled is a tree of life" (Prov. 13:2, NLT).

B: Become aware.

The second step, the "B," is to *become* aware of the stress that comes with loss.

Back in 1967, psychiatrists Thomas Holmes and Richard Rahe developed a questionnaire called the Social Readjustment Rating Scale (SRRS) for identifying major stressful life events. Each one of the forty-three stressful life events was awarded a Life Change Unit, depending on how traumatic a large sample of participants felt it to be.[4]

This inventory is commonly referred to as the Holmes-Rahe Life Stress Inventory. Over the years, it has been used to analyze how much a person can take before he or she falls apart.

Here are a few examples of the stressful life events in the questionnaire, along with the numeric value of their impact on a person:[5]

100—Loss of spouse
73—Divorce
65—Separation
53—Personal illness
50—Marriage
47—Getting fired
45—Retiring
40—Getting pregnant
36—Job change
26—Changing living conditions
17—Mortgage and loans
16 – Changing sleeping habits
12—Holidays

---

4. Dr. Saul McLeod, Stress and Life Events, SimplyPsychology, 2010, https://www.simplypsychology.org/SRRS.html.
5. Ibid.

If you total the points, here are the implications for physical health, mental health, and well-being:[6]

- 150 points or fewer—Means the person has a low susceptibility to stress and grief and a low to moderate chance of becoming ill in the near future.
- 150–300 points—The person has a 50 percent chance of health breakdown in the next two years.
- 300 points or more—There is an 80 percent chance of health breakdown in the next two years.

So someone who gets married in December, then visits the in-laws during the holidays after getting fired and changing jobs is in a highly stressful time!

Be aware of the situations you find yourself in. Understand the impact they can have on you. It's part of the healing process of handling hurt.

C. Know that cynicism is nearby.

The third step, "C," is about how *cynicism* comes around the corner when we are in emotional, physical, or spiritual defeat. Andrew Byers's book *Faith without Illusions* speaks about how hurt and grief can lead to cynicism. Byers defines cynicism as an "embittered disposition of distrust born out of painful disillusionment."[7]

What does this mean?

Byers starts by saying cynicism is "embittered disposition of distrust."

Where does this "distrust" originate from? Byers's answer is that cynicism comes out of a "painful disillusionment."

What *painful disillusionment* in your life has created distrust? What has left you in an "embittered disposition?" You've heard some of the reasons:

- "My pastor embarrasses me in front of the rest of the staff on a regular basis."
- "My spouse left me."

6. Ibid.
7. Andrew Byers, *Faith without Illusions: Following Jesus as a Cynic-Saint* (Westmont, Illinois: Intervarsity Press; 2011), 9.

- "My best friend had an affair with my wife."

Byers writes, "To be cynical is to be spiritually ill. But it is not terminal."[8]

When our souls get beaten up and scarred, eventually, cynicism and disillusionment settle in. This often results in isolation. We might get embittered and then distrust people. We may distrust God. This was certainly Job's dilemma. He was in a lot of pain: "My inward parts are in turmoil and never still; days of affliction come to meet me" (Job 30:27, ESV).

Job was cynical at times about God's mercy and justice and about His apparent distance from Job's situation. However, the bright spot is that Job was willing to get quiet and listen to the whisper of God. In Job 6:24, he prays, "Teach me, and I will be silent..." (ESV).

In the midst of grieving, Job prays to be teachable and silent, even though he wrestles with God's silence: "When he is quiet, who can condemn? When he hides his face, who can behold him, whether it be a nation or a man?" (Job 34:29, ESV).

Be prepared to battle some cynicism along the way. But do not despair because there is a solid diagnosis to help us wrestle with these detractors and distractors.

D. Receive your diagnosis from Scripture.
The fourth step of the grief stage, "D," is to see a *diagnosis* from God's Word.

In the Bible, Jesus demonstrates the importance of grieving. In John 11, we see that His friend, Lazarus, has died. Jesus shows up a bit late to the wake and weeps over losing his buddy, even though Jesus knows Lazarus is going to be raised from the dead. Martha wants to know what took Jesus so long to get to Lazarus. A little Jewish guilt trip from Martha to the Messiah, huh?

"Your brother *will rise* again," Jesus tells Martha.

"Jesus wept" is the classic Sunday school memory verse for little children (Job 11:35). We know from Scripture that Jesus deeply loved Lazarus (Job 11:36). Imagine being the Son of God (I know, tough

---

8. Ibid.

concept). You have arrived, and Lazarus is dead. He was your friend, and you cry intensely.

But your plan is to raise your pal from the dead. If the Lord Jesus cried over Lazarus, knowing fully well that Lazarus would come back to life within a few moments, I think it is safe to say we can grieve our losses. By the way, years later after dying and being raised by Jesus, Lazarus would die again. Twice! He has some stories to tell in heaven.

Isaiah 53:4 refers to the Messiah as "a man of sorrows and acquainted with grief."

Jesus understands grief more than you and I will ever know. In the Garden of Gethsemane, Jesus was so afflicted with grief that the Gospel of Matthew says, "My soul is overwhelmed with sorrow to the point of death." (Matt. 26:38). Three times he begs the Father, "If it is possible, may this cup be taken from me." Jesus then prays, "Yet not as I will, but as you will." (Matt. 26:39).

Jesus knows your pain, suffering, and grief. He has been there: "During the days of Jesus' life on earth, he offered up prayers and petitions with fervent cries and tears to the one who could save him from death, and he was heard because of his reverent submission" (Hebr. 5:7).

Jesus is our high priest who sympathizes with our weaknesses (Hebr. 4:15).

The Bible is full of people who grieved. Lamenting s normative for the human condition, and we have seen so many godly people in the Scriptures grieving over a loss: Abraham, Jacob, Solomon, David, Ruth, Josiah, John the Baptizer, Jesus, Paul, and others. "Blessed are those who mourn, for they shall be comforted" (Matt. 5:4).

King David composes a psalm of lament in 2 Samuel 1 for Saul and his son, Jonathan. All of us will suffer and experience times of grief.

The Merriam-Webster dictionary says *lament*, the verb, is "to express sorrow, regret, or unhappiness about something." Pastor Mark Vroegop says *lament* is "prayer in pain that leads to trust." He writes, "Lament typically asks at least two questions. One: Where are you, God? Two: If you love me, why is this happening?"[9]

9. Mark Vroegop, *Dark Clouds, Deep Mercy: Discovering the Grace of Lament* (Wheaton, Illinois: Crossway, 2019), 29.

Grieving is not a sign of weakness.

The apostle Paul speaks of his grief in 2 Corinthians, chapters 11–12. He shares his great sufferings, commonly referred to as his "thorn in the flesh" or "thorn in the side." Paul speaks of an agony so great he *begged God three times* to get rid of it, and God said no. Some scholars believe Paul's grief could be the result of emotional and mental wear and tear of serving Christ. Others think Paul had physical afflictions, like eye problems, or even knee and back issues. Paul wanted this thorn to be gone!

Lamenting is good. It's godly. Lamenting is very biblical and extremely human. To grieve is Christ-like. God told Paul that no matter how weak he felt, "My *grace is sufficient* for you, for my power is made perfect in weakness" (2 Cor. 12:9). Paul sought the best he could to celebrate in Christ's suffering. He's a lot more spiritual than most of us!

What you *do* with your grief matters. Grieving a loss is really a strength.

"God strengthens those who mourn" (Ps. 147:3). There is something powerful about those in grief. God says He will comfort the brokenhearted. Even when you and I are in the valley of the shadow of death, God promises to comfort us (Ps. 23:4). God is with you in the valleys and on the mountaintops. God's goodness is all around us. It's only when bad things come at us that His "goodness" comes into question. Even in your darkest valley, his rod and staff will comfort you.

Toward the end of the book of Job, Job comes to see that none of his losses had anything to do with him *personally*. All the suffering was beyond his control. Job started out as a victim, but by the end of the book, he chose not to have a victim mentality; rather, he was a victor. Job allowed the presence and love of God to sweep over his soul.

Your grief might still lead you to unanswered questions and to ponder God's silence. C. S. Lewis put words to his grief after losing his wife, Joy. He wondered where God was:

> "This is one of the most disquieting symptoms. When you are happy—so happy that you have no sense of needing Him, so happy that you are tempted to feel His claims upon you as an interruption— if you remember yourself and turn to Him with gratitude and praise, you will be—or so it feels—welcomed with open arms. But go to Him when your need is desperate, when all other help is vin, and

what do you find? A door slammed in your face, and a sound of bolting and double bolting on the inside. *After that, silence.* You may as *well turn away. The longer you wait, the more emphatic the silence will become. There are no lights in the windows. It might be an empty house. Was it ever inhabited? It seemed so once.*"[10]

Hurt and grief lead us to ponder the mystery of silence and the suspense that garners it.

Big Takeaway: Prayer: Father, teach me how to grieve my losses. Teach me to surrender those feelings. Enlarge my spirit during this time of grief, and help me listen well to You. Amen.

Questions for Reflection
1. How do hurt and grief distract you in your spiritual life?
2. What are some ways to handle periods of grief and hurt as they relate to God's silence?
3. What have been some helpful ways to navigate hurt and grief as you seek to be quiet before God?
4. In what ways do you relate to Job and his troubles? Explain.
5. What is your big takeaway from this chapter on hurt and grief?

---

10. C. S. Lewis, *A Grief Observed.*

PART THREE

THE MOST DIFFICULT QUESTION: HOW TO HANDLE GOD'S SILENCE?

"I know that He exists. Somewhere in silence."
—Emily Dickinson

K ing David was known as the man after God's own heart. In the psalms, we see King David asking the question no one wants to raise: Why is God silent? He is not alone. It's a question we ask today. Here are other examples from the Bible of this same type of musing:

- Psalm 22 starts with the prophetic words, "My God, my God, why have you forsaken me?"
- Psalm 44:2–23 asks, "Why do you sleep?"
- Psalm 109:1 says, "My God, whom I praise, do not remain silent, for people who are wicked and deceitful have opened their mouths against me…"

In Part 3, we ask the question, "How to handle God's silence?" *I believe that if and when God speaks, there is purpose and intentionality to it.* It is the same with God's silence—there is something ultimately meaningful about it. God's silence had a trigger point to it with King David, and it also does with us. It is a question we can no longer ignore.

Why is it so hard to wait on God? What do we do when we want certainty but only seem to have mystery?

Let's talk about it.

CHAPTER ELEVEN

WHY IS WAITING PAINFUL?

"In the silence of the heart God speaks. If you face God in prayer and silence, God will speak to you. Then you will know that you are nothing. It is only when you realize your nothingness, your emptiness, that God can fill you with Himself. Souls of prayer are souls of great silence."
—Mother Teresa

I t's hard to wait.

Ever stood in a long grocery line? Waited in the doctor's office for two hours for a routine visit? Stopped in gridlocked five o'clock traffic? Got to work late because you spilled coffee on your new shirt? Of course. Most of us hate to wait. It feels like forever.

Many of these scenarios are just short-term inconveniences.

When Rhonda and I waited on and off for more than a decade to see if we were going to have a second child or not, we learned quickly what causes us to be impatient: *expectations*.

Expectations and Parenting

As Andrew grew each year, so did our level of expectation. Sometimes we lowered them; other times we lifted the bar. For example, we noticed that during Andrew's toddler years, we had to speak slower. And during his teenager years, his listening skills improved each year, and he was better able to understand our fast talking.

We had to leverage our understanding of Down syndrome, decide what was appropriate for Andrew, and not compare him with other kids with Downs or other disabilities. What he could do and what our daughter,

Rachel, could do were entirely different.

When Andrew was three, we observed that he was a fish in the water—he loved to swim. He had no fear of the water. So we enrolled him in swim lessons. Before we knew it, he was competing in Special Olympics and eventually on the swim team in high school. He could do flips off the diving board and flip turns in swimming competitions—something I have never been able to do.

Andrew also started becoming proficient in paddleboarding in middle and high school and won several competitions. The more he won, the more we expected him to win. That is how expectations work. They can help us shoot for the moon. They can also let us down. Andrew has exceeded our hopes and dreams in so many ways. He can read at a tenth-grade level, and he loves books about animals. Have I mentioned he is an animal expert?

Andrew has no enemies. Everybody walks away from him being encouraged. He is a quasi-psychologist—he knows how to ask people questions about themselves, and they leave feeling valued. My friend, Corey, a former college and professional football player, says to me, "It must be fun waking up to Andrew's smile and joyful spirit." It is.

Andrew's innocence is so refreshing—he has no judgment of people, no matter what race, color, creed, religion, or origin. No matter what they think or do. He loves people, period!

Culture of Impatience

Our culture is a prime culprit of creating both *expectations* and *dissatisfaction!* Inventions like the laptop, internet, and iPhone have cultivated a desire for *immediate* satisfaction, which leads to our sinful nature of major *frustration and irritations* when things move slowly.

We want quick results, instant gratification, and fast relief. We live in a culture of instant facts, trivia, newscast, sports news, and Twitter posts. The endless information available on our phones keeps us preoccupied.

We go to Amazon.com and order our toothbrushes, grill cleaner, two new books, vitamins, safety goggles, lawnmowers, bedroom furniture, vacuum cleaners, and leaf blowers. They arrive quickly. When there is a delay, we get frustrated. Why is it taking so long to arrive?

We live in an instant-access culture. Everything in our culture is about speed.

Google something, and you can get the answer in seconds.

We want God to do the same: "I need you Lord, *now!*" We want *immediacy! That is our mantra.*

We live in a digital age that produces things super quickly. This causes problems when it comes to listening to God's voice and desiring God to "show up." We don't like waiting, do we? How do we embrace our limits and learn to wait?

As John Mark Comer suggests, the noise and pace of the world we live in don't help, either:

> The noise of the modern world makes us deaf to the voice of God, drowning out the one input we most need. I mean, how do we have any kind of spiritual life at all if we can't pay attention longer than a goldfish? How do you pray, read the Scriptures, sit under a teaching at church, or rest well on the Sabbath when every chance you get, you reach for the dopamine dispenser that is your phone?[1]

Delays Are Not Fun

One of the first concepts we learned from the special-needs community about Down syndrome was about delays when it comes to cognitive learning challenges. Our first speech therapist told us that many kids who have Down syndrome are really smart; it just takes them longer to learn things sometimes. Our first speech therapist, Debbie, explained that sometimes the brain of a kid with Down syndrome takes extra time to connect the dots.

"Just be patient," she would tell us. "Think of driving on the highway and experiencing a traffic jam, a wreck, road construction, or some other kind of delay. Andrew will have those kinds of delays in his life."

It took Andrew longer than most of his peers at school to learn how to spell, write, and learn the basics of life. It took him until middle school and early high school to fully know how to take care of his essential needs

---

1. John Mark Comer, *The Ruthless Elimination of Hurry: How to Stay Emotionally Healthy and Spiritually Alive in the Chaos of the Modern World* (Colorado Springs: Waterbrook, 2019), 122.

like brushing his teeth, dressing, using the toilet, and using a microwave.

The Bible talks much about delays and waiting, and it certainly impacts our relationship with people and *with God*. Much of waiting is short term. Compare it with the plight of the Israelites—*four hundred years* of waiting for God to deliver them from the hands of Egyptian slavery. Waiting and waiting and waiting. Wonder if the Hebrew people were counting the days, months, and years? Even after God freed them, the Israelites were not welcomed into the land of Canaan immediately.

They camped at the base of the mountain and waited *another* forty days.

The people of God grew impatient and frustrated, and eventually they made a really poor choice—they rejected the God of their forefathers. None of us likes waiting because we *love* control, yet the reality is that none of us has control over certain circumstances.

The Hebrew concept of waiting was *not passive resistance*. It was anticipation of God moving and putting things in their proper place and order. It was *active reliance*.

There is a condition to waiting, and it's called timing. The Hebrew view of time was that God is the clockmaker. He knows the times and purposes for each of our lives. King David expresses his anticipation of God coming to aid him: "But you, Lord, do not be far from me. You are my strength; come quickly to help me" (Ps. 22:19).

You can see the urgency in David's words: "Do not be far from me... come quickly." There is a sense that David knows God can come quickly. He also knows God's timing is not his own. It just seems slow because His timing and our timing have different clocks! My son, Andrew, says, "Waiting and fun should not be in the same sentence." How true!

God is working as we wait. There is *purpose* behind the waiting.

We have waited, but have we waited *patiently*? Not too often. I have certainly waited *impatiently!* In Psalm 5:3, David prayed, "In the morning I lay my requests before you and wait expectantly."

In the Scriptures, waiting is not passive; it's active.

Waiting: Psalms and Jesus

Psalm 40 and Isaiah 40 both mention waiting. This has been a classic verse people memorize or put on a coffee mug: "They who wait for the

Lord will gain new strength" (Isa. 40:31, NASB).

We love that verse, right? Except when we are forced into a time of waiting!

> "For God alone, O my soul, wait in silence, for my hope is from him."
> —Psalm 62:5, ESV

> "Be *still* before the Lord and wait patiently for him."
> —Psalm 37:7, ESV

Waiting is giving God some room and space to speak.

As Jesus approached the final verdict of Pilate on whether he would be crucified, He must have felt nervous anticipation about His final steps to the cross. He was in a period of waiting.

Four Essentials for Waiting Patiently

May I ask you, what are you waiting for? What specific goal or dream are you waiting to see happen? A new job, a new relationship, a new home, or a new purpose? It's easy to read about Elijah and Jesus waiting, but what about us? How do we meet God if we have trouble waiting?

In the New Testament, James 1:1–5 provides some perspective on how to get you through the messiest and hardest situations. Here are *four essentials* for navigating uncertain times and learning how to get a grip on patiently waiting on God.

Essential #1: Train your brain.

James was the half-brother of Jesus; they grew up in the same household. James did not believe in Jesus as Messiah until a remarkable event—the resurrection of Jesus. Jesus appeared to more than five hundred people, and 1 Corinthians 15:7 mentions one little fact: *"Then he appeared to James,* then to all the apostles." I guess hearing from your brother who was once dead and now alive would be a pretty convincing reason to start believing that He was the Messiah!

In his letter, James begins by identifying himself not as the brother of Jesus, but rather as a servant: "James, a servant of God and of the Lord Jesus Christ...Greetings" (James 1:1).

Then he continues his practical book about trials and tests, telling us they come in many different shapes and sizes. Most importantly, trials have divine purposes for our lives: "Consider it pure joy, my brothers and sisters, whenever you face trials of many kinds, because you know that the testing of your faith produces perseverance. Let perseverance finish its work so that you may be mature and complete, not lacking anything. If any of you lacks wisdom, you should ask God, who gives generously to all without finding fault, and it will be given to you" (James 1:1–7).

James gives us an indication of what to do when we are waiting on God.

When we are in an impatient mood, James tells us to make a mental adjustment. I call this training your brain. James states that life is hard and will confront our faith. Remind yourself that just around the corner, some type of trials and tests will spring up that will challenge your faith! It's kind of like coaching yourself. Do you ever talk to yourself? Sure you do. James is telling us to talk to ourselves with these words: "When troubles of any kind come your way, consider it an opportunity for great joy" (James 1:2, NLT).

James does not say *if* troubles come, but *when* they come. He tells us to train our brains—to adjust our minds and attitudes, to enter each day knowing that we are going to have to wait out some good and bad situations. "Count it all joy," James says, knowing that good will come from these experiences. The Message version says trials are a "sheer *gift.*" "We will be tested with them from all sides."

I admit, life presents situations that I don't know what to do about it. Therefore, I say these axioms daily:

- I will see trials as a gift to grow me.
- God is trying to work out something good in my life.
- I will train my brain to be patient in the process of waiting.

So that's the first essential—to prepare ourselves for trials with joy. To train our brains. The Living Bible says, "Dear brothers, is your life full of difficulties and temptations? Then be happy, for when the way is rough, your patience has a chance to grow" (James 1:2–3).

Essential # 2: Don't bail.

The second essential is that we recognize that the testing of our faith "produces perseverance" (James 1:3). James's advice when waiting is this: don't quit. Don't bail when things get hard. "So let it grow, and don't try to squirm out of your problems. For when your patience is finally in bloom, then you will be ready for anything, strong in character, full and complete" (James 1:4-5, TLB).

Something good will come out of this mess. "Don't squirm out" of your situation. Hang in there, no matter how difficult the situation is, no matter how much waiting is involved. Know that God will bring something real and powerful out of your life.

If you hate waiting, just *admit* it. But don't hit the eject button too soon. Tell God your sob story. Get it off your chest. If you need to pout, let it out. God can handle it. If you want to whine and complain, go ahead for a few minutes, maybe for a couple of hours. The Israelites deserve a master's degree in complaining!

After you have grumbled, recognize it is time to move forward. God knows what you are thinking and feeling. Maybe you are wondering, "Why should I even want to be resilient and not throw in the towel?" James gives us a key reason why: "For you know that when your faith is tested, your *endurance* has a chance to grow" (James 1:3, NLT). When we exercise, we use muscles and make them work. As we test our strength, the muscles also learn endurance. It's the same way with resilience.

I love James 1:4: "Let perseverance *finish* its work…"

The word *perseverance* means to "abide under." ESV uses the word "steadfastness." God uses the times of waiting to produce endurance in you! My friend, David, who teaches Greek New Testament, says it has this kind of rendering: "Let perseverance complete its work…so you will be complete."

What work is James talking about? *Completeness. Maturity.*

Maturity and completeness do not happen according to James, through memorizing the Bible, by loving people who are hard to love, or trying to obey the Ten Commandments. Becoming complete happens through… drum roll…

Perseverance—persevering during the hard times, through times of waiting, and in those days when God seems silent.

Let perseverance finish its work—the work of maturation.

Think about the life of Saul, whose name was changed to Paul. We call him "the apostle Paul" today. The former persecutor of the church, a religious Pharisee, and the prominent writer of most of the New Testament knew persecution, oppression, and injustice firsthand. Paul knew the pressures of waiting and suffering.

The risen Christ appeared to him with a vision on the Damascus Road, and he needed to get his theology and heart realigned. Following his coming to Jesus, he went off to be alone in Arabia for *three years* as he processed all that had happened to him (see Galatians 1:17).

Following his time in Arabia, Paul went fully armored to speak, teach, and be a disciple for the Kingdom of God. And it did not always have pleasant results. He would face beatings. He was flogged and put in prison: "Three times I was beaten with rods. Once I was stoned, three times I was shipwrecked, I spent a night and a day in the open sea, I have been constantly on the move. I have been in danger from rivers, in danger from bandits, in danger from my own countrymen, in danger from Gentiles, in danger in the city, in danger in the country, in danger at sea, and in danger from false brothers" (2 Corin. 11:25–26).

In spite of all the hardships, which included thirst, going without food, being cold and naked, Paul was still caring for the Christians he shepherded and the lost he wanted to reach. Paul learned to "endure patiently," as it states in Revelation 3:10.

Paul was becoming more whole, mature, and complete as he persevered. And perseverance has an outcome: growth. Who we are *becoming* while we wait is more vital than what we are waiting for. Let perseverance complete its work.

Essential #3: Keep on growing.

James concludes his short essay on how to patiently wait on God. He writes, "so that you may be *mature* and complete, not lacking anything" (James 1:4–5).

Maturity is an experience that happens through endurance and perseverance. Waiting is what helps us sink our roots deeply into the soil of Christ. Unfortunately, some Christ-followers never get to this place of maturity because they have not tried to apply these truths.

God will not always change the circumstance we are in; He does want to change us. It's like when my son, Andrew, was born. We had to endure the unknown—what would his life be like? Would he walk? Talk? Thankfully, yes to both of those questions. God changed us, not our situation. We had to persevere. Andrew had to persevere, and this brought maturity.

One of my favorite shows is *American Ninja Warrior.* What is incredible to me isn't the feats they exhibit on the climbing walls, or the moving twists and turns; rather, it is their personal stories about how they got on the show. Many of these athletes have some kind of disability, disease, or hardship. Some have had multiple heart attacks, Parkinson's disease, diabetes; substance abuse, eating disorders, and other issues that affect them physically, emotionally, and spiritually.

Amazing things happen often to people who do not quit! Apostle Paul writes about *perseverance* in Romans 5:3–4: "Not only so, but we glory in our sufferings, because we know that suffering produces perseverance; perseverance, character; and character, hope."

Perseverance...the ability to endure under the most intense times of distress and pain. Perseverance produces character, and character produces hope. Romans 15:4 tells us everything that was stated in the past was "written to teach us, so that through *endurance* taught in the Scriptures and the encouragement they provide we might have *hope*."

Perseverance during those difficult, messy waiting times provides *hope* that God is still working behind the scenes. He who has begun a good work will complete it as we persevere. And where does this perseverance come from, you ask? "May the *God who gives endurance* and encouragement give you the same attitude of mind toward each other that Christ Jesus had" (Rom. 15:5).

God gives us endurance. It's not natural; it's supernatural. As *we endure, we mature.*

Jesus wants us to grow into *spiritual and emotional maturity,* which is measured by how well we *persevere* during hard times. Not through memorizing Bible trivia, fasting extra days, or giving food to the homeless, although those are all good things.

Maturity is measured not by performance but by perseverance. And because God gives you perseverance as a gift, you don't have to rely on your own will power or a "pick yourself up by the bootstraps" mentality.

Essential #4: Ask for wisdom.

"If any of you *lacks wisdom*, you should *ask God*, who gives
generously to all without finding fault, and it will be given to you."
—James 1:5, NIV

"If you need wisdom, ask our generous God, and he will give it to you."
—James 1:5, NLT

The fourth and final essential for learning to wait patiently is to ask God for wisdom. When you have no idea what to do, James says to "ask our generous God." Notice the promise: "He will give it to you."

Wisdom is the ability to see life's circumstances from God's perspective, with a larger view, from a broader context: "Get *wisdom*; get insight; do not forget, and do not turn away from the words of my mouth. Do not forsake her, and she will keep you; love her, and she will guard you" (Prov. 4:5–6, ESV).

What to do…when you don't know what to do? What do you do when waiting is tough and even unbearable? Ask for wisdom. What is your decision? These four essentials are available as you read these words. Get started. Today. You might just experience His voice in the waiting.

Big Takeaway: How do you learn to wait on God? Train your brain to be joyful, knowing that hardships are right around the corner. Keep rowing the boat. Don't bail. Endure. Persevere.

Questions for Reflection
1. On a scale of 1 to 10 (1 being poor and 10 being great), where do you typically fall on the scale of being able to wait patiently? Explain.
2. What are some the areas of your life in which you find it hardest to be patient?

3. What are some current issues you are facing which needs some perseverance and mental toughness?
4. What steps do you need to take when it comes to applying the four essentials to navigating patient waiting?

CHAPTER TWELVE
EMBRACING MYSTERY WHEN CERTAINTY FADES

"I must say that when I go to church, and I do go to church, I ponder the mystery. I meditate on the 'why' of 'why people are as they are' and why 'bad things happen to good people' and 'why good things happen to bad people...' The mystery is what I think is, almost, the grand unifying theory of all mankind."
—Tom Hanks

It took me more than twenty years to write this book. In fact, it was never in my thought process until my secretary suggested it when Andrew turned three years old. I was not ready. Not enough life experience under my belt. Too immature. I needed time to think through the issues of suffering, silence, special needs, doubt, and all the factors that contribute to people growing in the faith or drifting from it.

After we discovered Andrew had Down syndrome, I felt uncertainty about his life and worried about our family as we ventured into this new phase of life. Leading our family into the world of special needs was not part of the written script in my mind. On top of that, I also had the pressure of leading my university students and staff, doing speaking engagements, and running my side coaching business.

Also, encouraging and helping Rhonda as she faced cancer was a complex matter. In addition, trying to navigate life with our daughter, Rachel, as she transitioned from high school to college was, at times, very *uncertain*. We were parenting a young adult through and after college with a toddler at home. We were about to raise two "only" children!

I felt the pressure from myself and others to know for certain what I was doing, and sometimes that just wasn't possible. People looked to me for certainty, and sometimes finding clarity for one day at a time was all I could muster.

We all want certainty, don't we? It's the one thing people want from politicians, leaders, and parents. It's the one thing people want from us that few can deliver!

Desiring Certainty

When it comes to a relationship with God and with people, most are looking for some kind of hope and certainty. Unfortunately, some end up discouraged because this expectation does not seem to have sustaining power.

My friend, Dr. Fuzz Rana, is an apologetics expert, meaning he can get people to consider the claims of God's existence. People have gone from being atheists or agnostics to believing there is a God because of Fuzz's great passion and knowledge. He has used science and mystery to convince people that God is real, but he cannot "prove" to them 100 percent of the time, with certainty, that God exists.

Mystery is undersold in the Christian movement.

We do not embrace mystery enough because we like topics dealing with truth so we can have a nice, happy ending. We don't want a book's last chapter to leave us with the bow untied. We don't like uncertainty.

When I was dating Rhonda, I wanted certainty that she was the *one*. One day I told her, "I believe God told me that we are going to be married someday."

She said, "That's nice. God has not told me."

Ouch.

Eventually, she saw the light! We dated for eight months, were engaged for eleven months, and have been married since the dinosaur age!

My Top Ten Strategies for Dealing with Uncertainty

Here are my top ten ways to consider the issues of certainty when we feel God is absent. How do we "keep on keeping on" when certainty fades? I hope these suggestions will be a great help to you on the journey of faith, wrestling with noise and the tension of mystery and silence.

1. Embrace your life of faith as both mystery and truth.

God establishes His truth through His written Word, called "words of this law," that are given to us: *"The secret things* belong to the Lord our God, but the things revealed belong to us and to our children forever, that we may follow all the *words of this law"* (Deut. 29:29).

Scripture, "the words of this law," is our standard for life and faith. This is the "truth" of the faith.

There are however, many mysteries to the Bible that we do not understand. That is why theologians have argued about certain texts for centuries; we all have different interpretations of what the Bible verses mean. And of course, most of us think *our view* is the correct one. Some people just want the truth. Others want mystery. It's not either/or; it's both/*and.* Let truth and mystery be part of the whole system.

Deuteronomy 29:29 addresses not only the *truth of God* through His Word, which belongs to us and our children, but Moses and his peeps mention "the *secret* things belong to the Lord."

What do the *secret things* refer to? The "secret things" are those things *only* God knows. These are facts, truths, and mysteries that are only in God's wheelhouse, beyond our human comprehension.

Sometimes, God discloses secrets. In fact, Jeremiah the prophet says, "Call to me and I will answer you, and I will tell you great and *hidden things* that *you have not* known" (33:3, ESV).

I actually love the idea that there are mysteries that are beyond me. Moses called them "secrets," and Jeremiah refers to these mysteries as "hidden things" that "you have not known."

Secrets. Hidden Things.

Only in God's closet.

Sometimes, God will reveal these mysteries to us; other times, not. Proverbs 25:2 says, "It is the glory of God to conceal a matter; to search out a matter is the glory of kings."

In God's glory, He conceals some matters. *Conceal* means to "hide, keep from sight; prevent from being known or noticed." The glory of kings is to search for answers. God does not have to search for new answers and understanding, like we do.

Mystery is wondering about why things happen. We want to know. We want to know why God does things. And why He doesn't do other things.

Mystery is good for the soul. It keeps us speculating and questioning. Mystery is very Christian. Godly. Don't be afraid of mystery.

Embrace both truth and mystery.

2. Recognize that God's voice is in the wonder of silence.

Explorer and author Erling Kagge knows the reality of silence firsthand. Kagge was the first person to complete the Three Poles Challenge on foot—the North Pole, the South Pole, and the summit of Mount Everest. Here is what he writes in his book, *Silence: In the Age of Noise:*[1]

> Not long ago, I tried to convince my three daughters that the world's secrets are hidden inside silence…The girls looked at me skeptically. Surely silence is…nothing? Even before I was able to explain the way in which silence can be a friend, and a luxury more valuable than any of the Louis Vuitton bags they so covet, their minds had been made up: silence is fine to have on hand when you're feeling sad. Beyond that, it is useless.
>
> *Wonder is the very engine of life.* But my children are thirteen, sixteen, and nineteen years old and wonder less and less; if they still wonder at anything, they pull out their smartphones to find the answer. None of them had any interest in discussing the subject of silence, so in order to invoke it, I told them about two friends of mine who decided to climb Mount Everest. Early one morning they left base camp to climb the southwest wall of the mountain. It was going well. Both reached the summit, but then came the storm. They soon realized they would not make it down alive. The first got a hold of his pregnant wife via satellite phone. Together they decided on the name of the child that she was carrying.
>
> Then he quietly passed away just below the summit. My other friend was not able to contact anyone before he died. No one knows exactly what happened on the mountain in those hours. Thanks to the dry, cool climate 8,000 meters above sea level, they have both been freeze-dried. They lie there in silence, looking no different, more or less, from the way they were last time I saw them, twenty-

---

1. Erling Kagge, *Silence: In the Age of Noise* (New York: Vintage Books, 2018), 2–3.

two years ago. For once there was silence around the table.

David—shepherd boy turned king and psalm writer—continually brings up the topic of God's silence in the Bible. He lets it all hang out. He doubts, screams, cries, freaks out, laughs, questions, stresses, gets angry, and is depressed. He epitomizes the ebbs and flows of a human wanting to meet God. And David ponders one big question:

"Why are you silent?"

"My God, do not remain silent. Do not be deaf to me."

God speaks in silence. Receive the gift of God's silence. In the psalms, David suggests that God often dwells in silence. The wonder of silence and solitude.

Henry Nouwen writes, "In solitude I get rid of my scaffolding: no friends to talk with, no telephone calls to make, no meetings to attend, no music to entertain, no books to distract, just me—naked, vulnerable, weak, sinful, deprived, broken—nothing…Solitude is the place of the great struggle and the great encounter…It is the place where Christ remodels us in his own image and frees us from the victimizing compulsions of the world."[2]

3. Invite others into the journey—don't go solo.

Learning about being silent—more contemplative, more reflective—in our spiritual adventure is not about going solo all the time, but inviting others into the journey of silence and trust. When you experience something awesome, don't you want to welcome others into the experience? My friends went to a Trappist monastery a few years ago and had an amazing time. They didn't want to keep this place a secret. They shared the joy and encouraged me to go. I am so glad I did. It was a radical experience, and I will never be the same because of it.

Don't you want to share great experiences with someone else? The apostle Paul uses words like "encourage one another," "love one another," "bear one another's burdens." He wrote in 2 Corinthians 1:4 these words about God's comfort to us in hardships: "Praise be to the God and Father

2. Henri J. M. Nouwen, *Way of the Heart: Connecting with God Through Prayer, Wisdom, and Silence* (New York: Ballantine Books; 1981), 15,18.

of our Lord Jesus Christ, the Father of compassion and the God of all comfort, who comforts us in all our troubles."

God comforts us in tough times, but the Bible doesn't say how. The Father and Jesus come alongside us in some mysterious way. But we do get an indication about the *why* of comfort: "So that we can comfort those in any trouble with the comfort we ourselves have received" (2 Corin.1:4).

God comforts us so we can comfort others. God walks with us so we can walk with others. It's called *community*.

We become Jesus to others who are facing the same pain we have gone through. In fact, Jesus calls the Holy Spirit "the Comforter," which means to "come alongside." When we walk with people, we are coming alongside them during their times of highs and lows.

Share your story, no matter how hard it has been. Someone needs to hear it. Bring others into your narrative. Whether it's in the mountains or the valleys, let people into the journey. And when it comes to noise, doubts, distractions, and pain, don't always go solo.

4. Resist the idol of certainty.

Some believe faith is the absence of doubt and that faith must feel and affirm certainty 100 percent of the time.

Austin Fischer writes about this erroneous view of faith: "It's certainty or bust. There are a number of problems with this response, and the first is that we are humans, and humans cannot be certain about much of anything."[3]

Some call Hebrews 11 the "Hall of Fame of Faith." It chronicles how Abel, Abraham, Enoch, Noah, and others followed God in faith. A popular verse to quote is Hebrews 11:6: "It is impossible to please God without faith. Anyone who wants to come to him must believe that God exists and that he rewards those who sincerely seek him" (NLT).

Faith is the signature hallmark of this chapter. It has remarkable stories of men and women who perform tremendous acts for God: "By faith these people overthrew kingdoms, ruled with justice, and received what God had promised. They shut the mouths of lions, quenched the flames

---

3. Fischer, *Faith in the Shadows*, 20.

of fire, and escaped death by the edge of the sword." (Hebr. 11:34, NLT).

The story line however, is not all victorious: "Some were jeered at, and their backs were cut open with whips. Others were chained in prisons. Some died by stoning, some were sawed in half, and others were killed with the sword" (Hebr. 11:36–37, NLT).

The only mention of 100 percent certainty is their deaths—nothing else.

Austin Fischer says, "So while we often think admitting our doubt and uncertainty would damage our witness to the world, I am now convinced it would do the opposite. Owning our uncertainty does not make our faith less credible but more credible since it makes our faith more human and thus more honest. We need not overcome our humanity to have faith."[4]

Dr. Kate Bowler, a professor at Duke Divinity school, knows the issues of faith, mystery, and uncertainty. As I mentioned in chapter 6, she was diagnosed with stage IV colon cancer at the age of thirty-five. Her world began to spin out of control. She writes this about her experience:[5]

> Most everyone I meet is dying to make me certain. They want me to know, without a doubt, that there is a hidden logic to this seeming chaos. Even when I was still in the hospital, a neighbor came to the door and told my husband that everything happens for a reason.
>
> "I'd love to hear it," he replied.
>
> "Pardon?" she said, startled.
>
> "The reason my wife is dying," he said in that sweet and sour way he has, effectively ending the conversation as the neighbor stammered something and handed him a casserole.
>
> Christians want me to reassure them that my cancer is all part of a plan. A few letters even suggest that God's plan was that I get cancer so I could help people.

Kate Bowler knows pain, which is somewhat of an irony because she

4. Ibid.
5. Bowler, *Everything Happens for a Reason*, 112–113.

is an expert on the "prosperity gospel." Toward the end of her book, *Everything Happens for a Reason—And Other Lies I've Loved*, she has a section called "Absolutely *Never Say* This to People Experiencing Terrible Times: A Short List." Here is a brief excerpt:

> The only thing worse than saying this is pretending that you *know* the reason. I've had hundreds of people tell me the reason for my cancer. Because of my sin. Because of my unfaithfulness. Because God is fair. Because God is unfair. Because of my aversion to Brussels sprouts. I mean, no one is short of reasons. So if people tell you this, make sure you are there when they go through the cruelest moments of their lives, and start offering your own. When someone is drowning, the only thing worse than failing to throw them a lifesaver is handing them a reason.[6]

You may never be fully satisfied with the unknowns. That is okay because I am willing to bet that true, real, and radical faith leans into embracing mystery, not just certainty. You can be uncertain. You can resist the idol of certainty.

And when it comes down to listening to God, and experiencing His divine presence, certainty is good, but mystery will win in the end. Keep asking questions. Stay open, and be curious. Be inquisitive about the faith.

5. Be differentiated.

A *differentiated self* is language used in my study of family systems. It is the highest state of being, sort of like Maslow's hierarchy of living, called "self-actualization." Self- actualization deals with people's ability to choose their full potential, to be aware of what they need and what they don't need.

A *differentiated self* means you know *who you are and know who you are not*. Growth in this area involves the ability to separate yourself from other people's needs. A differentiated self, for example, knows how to use "I statements" instead of following the crowd by giving into the pressure

---

6. Ibid., 170.

of saying "we." A differentiated self chooses not to blame others and takes personal responsibility. A differentiated self rarely uses language like, "You made me do this." A highly differentiated self has an amazing amount of self-awareness. It tells me "who I am and who I'm not."

A differentiated person uses phrases like these:

- "I choose to love you, even if I don't like your actions."
- "I choose to accept mystery."
- "I choose to live with some ambiguity."
- "I choose to love God when I don't understand His ways."
- "I choose times of silence."
- "I choose the mystery of silence."
- "I choose to trust in God."
- "I choose to not lean unto my own understanding."
- "I choose to not understand all the mysteries of God and the universe."
- "I choose to accept my limitations as a human."
- "I choose to say yes, or no, depending on my needs and the needs of my family. I am not afraid to have boundaries and say no."
- "I can accept that God is mysterious and many things that happen are bizarre."

In a moving scene from the 2006 film *We Are Marshall*, Nate Ruffin is the quarterback who never got on the plane that would ultimately crash and kill all seventy-five players, staff, coaches, and boosters of the 1970 Marshall University football team. His life was spared, but his soul was in torment. He feels he should have been on that plane with his band of brothers.

Nate is crying, asking, "Why?" He leans on the shoulder of the head coach, played by Matthew McConaughey, and says, "That was my team. Why, coach?

The coach says, "I don't know, Nate. I don't know."

I love his answer. Sometimes we don't know the answers to life's most difficult questions.

A differentiated man or woman is a person who will be comfortable in his or her own skin, doubts or no doubts, stress or no stress, worries or at peace. A differentiated individual can admit, "I don't know" or "Yes, I believe this truth."

Become more differentiated in your faith.

6. Celebrate mystery; don't just tolerate it.

A few years ago, I heard a commencement speaker tell the college graduates, "As you get older, it's okay to become more comfortable with mystery over predictability." He explained that many of the graduates still had no idea where their future was headed, and they needed to take the pressure off themselves of having to have it all figured out in the next hour.

Why can't we allow mystery to be just that—a mystery?

There is a crazy passage in the Bible. Of course it's in the book of Revelation, and it speaks literally of the mystery of silence: "When the Lamb ripped off the seventh seal, Heaven fell quiet—*complete silence* for about half an hour" (8:1, MSG).

The NIV states, "When he opened the seventh seal, there was *silence in heaven* for about half an hour."

Silence in heaven, huh? This passage follows Revelation 7:17: "For the Lamb at the center of the throne will be their shepherd, he will lead them to springs of living water. And God will wipe away every tear from their eyes."

There have been all kinds of jokes about why there's thirty minutes of silence in heaven. Maybe you have heard some of them, too:

- "My dad was not there yet."
- "My sister did not get the announcement."
- "No women had arrived in heaven."
- "My aunt was escorted out because she talks too much."

I am not here for the purpose of doing a commentary on Revelation. But it's safe to say that following the huge gathering of worshippers in Revelation 7, praises and shouts of thanks and honor given to God, there enters a dramatic pause—silence in heaven.

A colossal hush!

Complete silence for about thirty minutes.

It strikes me in a similar fashion with the silence that happens before the final "Hallelujah" in the Chorus of Handel's Messiah. It reminds me of a sporting event when someone has tragically died, and before the national anthem, there is a collective "moment of silence."

I have a feeling that heaven will be a noisy place with worship of the Father, Son, and Holy Spirit. It will also have moments of worship through silence. The Lamb is worthy to praise with words and to be honored with silence.

Why is there silence in heaven for thirty minutes? What does this mean? I personally don't think anyone really knows.

Meanwhile, celebrate silence—don't just tolerate it.

7. Don't box Jesus in.

God is bigger than your theology box. For all the teachings listed in the Bible, I promise you will not be able to figure them all out. And when you think you have it nailed down, and you stuff them into your little box, Jesus will jump out of the box.

I've met people who can eloquently explain the doctrine of the Trinity; predestination; or the doctrine of hell, heaven, or prophecy. They have it down pat. The problem is: they really don't. They just think they do.

They are comfortable with *categories* but uncomfortable with *mystery*.

Can we please stop putting Jesus in our little boxes?

Maybe the *best* answer to people's suffering is to offer compassion and loving acts of kindness. Perhaps we need to show up to someone's house with a piping-hot pizza, salad, hot-fudge cake, and ice cream with smile, give them a hug, and leave.

Allow people to wrestle with the beauty, complexity, paradox, and simplicity of the faith. Be still. Stop controlling the narrative. Let God… be God.

When you encounter someone in a deep pit of discouragement, please don't rush to quote Scripture at them. At the right time, it may be appropriate. Be sensitive: "Gently encourage the stragglers, and reach out for the exhausted, pulling them to their feet. Be patient with each person, attentive to individual needs" (1 Thess. 5:13–15, MSG).

Be quiet and love them. Encourage. Be patient. And get rid of your boxes.

8. *Understand that it boils down to trust.*

Mystery and uncertainty boil down to one crucial element in a relationship with God: trust. Proverbs 3:5 tells us to trust Him and to "lean not" to our own understanding. I'm decent at the *trust* part of the passage, but I struggle with the *don't lean to our own understanding* piece.

Faith is about trust. It works not only in the religious realm, but pretty much in all areas of life. Trust is risk and courage cemented together. One of the most famous narratives in the Gospels is when Jesus calms the sea as the disciples are in the middle of a massive storm: "Suddenly a furious storm came up on the lake, so that the waves swept over the boat. "But Jesus was sleeping" (Matt. 8:24).

He was taking a siesta, perhaps snoring?

Ever felt like Jesus was *sleeping* in your stormy situation? How do you respond to this apparent disappearing act? As you just saw, the disciples had to *wake Jesus up* during their storm! The disciples actually demonstrated some initiative in waking Him up, knowing that Jesus had the power to deal with the situation.

The boat got swamped by a furious storm so massive, it was about to blow over the entire boat and everyone in it. A "squall" came onto the lake. A *squall* is a sudden, violent gust of wind that brings about a huge outpouring of wind and rain.

In the midst of facing personal storms, the wind might be blowing harshly. You may be in a storm of feelings and think, "God has left me all alone in this boat of suffering." God has not calmed your financial, spiritual, or emotional squall that you are right in the midst of—at least for now. Maybe you feel abandoned as you parent alone. Or your marriage is about to fracture. Perhaps you have an aging parent and don't know what to do. Your children have walked away from the faith while in college. Life is windy and stormy. The squall is enormous.

Is your boat about to sink? Remember, you cannot control the storm you are in. We can *choose trust* or disbelief.

When God is confusing or seems absent, you and I have a choice to make. A decision to follow through with. *I choose trust*, at least most of the time. Your circumstances are not in your control, and your emotions have thrown you down to the bottom of the boat in misery. Your feelings and insights are out of whack.

Back to that Scripture in Matthew—Jesus comes out of His sleep and tells the winds and raging storm to settle down. He utters only four words, in the form of a question. It may be the most important question in the midst of suffering: "You of little faith, why are you so afraid?" (Matt. 8:26).

In essence, He was asking, "Where is your faith?" (Or, in the Olshine translation, "Where is your *trust*?")

In the movie *We Bought a Zoo*, Benjamin Mee (played by Matt Damon) is wrestling with a series of life decisions after the death of his wife, Katherine. He makes a radical choice to quit his job as a journalist, leave the city of Los Angeles, and move with his two children to an eighteen-acre property formerly known as the Rosemoor Wildlife Park. The park still has wild animals: zebras, lions, tigers, and bears ("Oh my!").

One day, Benjamin is sitting with his teenage son and makes a profound statement: "Sometimes all you need is twenty seconds of insane courage. Just literally twenty seconds of embarrassing bravery, and I promise you something great will come of it."

When it comes to embracing silence and the mystery with it, and how God is involved in it, start with twenty seconds of trust. *Twenty seconds of insane courage.*

As you embrace the discipline of solitude and silence with a perspective of trust, courage, and risk, you can bank on the fact that "something great will come of it."

9. Identify your sweet spot.

Thomas à Kempis wrote the masterpiece called *The Imitation of Christ,* which evaluates the life of Jesus, how He lived, and how He modeled a way of life to us.

Imitate Christ and his ways. The rabbis had a phrase: "May you be covered in the dust of your rabbi." It meant that students, who would follow the Teacher all day long, would imitate the rabbi. By the end of the night, their sandals were covered in the dust of following the leader because the roads were dirty and dusty.

Sometimes, God speaks to us in uncomfortable spaces and places. Maybe going to the mountains and desert to get alone with God is not your "thang." Yet I know that you and I are unique. Each person has a unique calling. It's hardwired into your DNA.

It is through personal discovery, that whatever and wherever you find solitude and contentment, you are beginning to imitate the ways of Jesus. Some call it a "sweet spot." When I played high-school tennis, our coach used this phrase often. Your "sweet spot" is when you hit the ball perfectly, and there is a certain sound to it. It's a sweet sound. Baseball players and golfers talk about the sweet spot in their sports, too.

Most of us will hear and follow Jesus's voice in the areas we are gifted in. Our sweet spots. It's probably so intuitive that we do it without thinking. My friends say I make it look easy when I speak to small or large audiences composed primarily of middle- and high-school students. It's not that easy, but it has been my sweet spot for years.

"Stay in your lane" or "Find your calling" or "Discover your mission" are some phrases people use to encourage someone to listen to the voice of God. Find out what your mission is; you will be happy when you do.

My mission is simple: "To be a living witness for Jesus." Now, I am not a Bible thumper—I don't beat people up with the Bible, metaphorically speaking. I am not intrusive. I don't get in people's grills. However, I am constantly looking for connections and ways to share my faith and teach God's Word. I do however, like to knock on "doors" and try walking in.

I am a bridge builder. This is where I see and sense His voice when it comes to relationships, especially outside the church world.

A while back, I needed a physical at my doctor's office, so I made an appointment. When I arrived, my nurse took my blood pressure and pulse, and she looked upset. I asked her if she was okay, and she said, "No. I *hate* my husband."

The venom began to pour out of her mouth. I was taken aback with her honesty, and she proceeded for the next five minutes to blast her husband. I listened and then asked, "Can I pray with you?" She agreed, and I prayed for God to restore her marriage.

She left, and the doctor came in later. I never did find out if my blood pressure was good or not.

Three months later, I had my follow-up visit. When I arrived, I was escorted into a room, and moments later a nurse popped in. It was that same nurse. She said, "Hey, counselor, do you remember me? You prayed over my marriage."

"Yes, I remember you. Well, how's it going?"

She said, "You are not going to believe it. God answered your prayer. My marriage is better than ever. About three days after you prayed, my husband started to change. His attitude and countenance was so different. I'm so grateful—thank you. Your prayer saved our marriage. It worked!"

"You are welcome. That is exciting for you two. Thanks for sharing that with me."

Then she said, "And guess what? Three weeks ago, we found out I'm *pregnant.*"

"Congratulations! Well, I had nothing to do with that," I said, which, of course, she already knew.

She laughed. That time, she told me my blood pressure was fine.

God uses us. He puts us in the right place at the right time. We experience the voice of God through our sweet spot. Act on it. It's almost supernaturally natural. Jesus is in your sweet spot. Find it. Use it.

10. Embrace ambiguity and the mystery of silence as a lifestyle.
Dictionary.com defines *ambiguity* as "doubtfulness or uncertainty of meaning or intention."

We need to become content with some of the things we don't know or will never know. Maybe you have heard the phrase, "We don't know what we don't know." Becoming comfortable in our own skin means allowing mystery to be a mystery! And allowing the mystery of silence to be a… mystery!

Let stillness and silence be what it can be—a mystery that is also meant to be an experience. A stillness that can produce peace and contentment. A. J. Swoboda writes, "At times in the Christian journey, we will be given the gift of God's silence in the face of immeasurable challenge."[7]

The gift of God's silence is not always something we want, but it most certainly is something we need.

Jesus asked the disciples, "You do not want to leave, too, do you?"

Peter said, "Lord, to whom shall we go?" (John 6:67). When life stinks, and stuff hits the fan, sometimes all we have left is Jesus.

7. A. J. Swoboda, *After Doubt: How to Question Your Faith without Losing It* (Grand Rapids, Michigan: Brazos Press, 2021), 114.

Where else can we go?

A. J. Swoboda continues, "To look lovingly on Jesus, however, is to press in even when he's silent—when it seems he is ignoring you. God's Word isn't the only thing that we believe to be inspired. His silence is too...If we can never understand his silence, we'll certainly never understand his words."[8]

My son, Andrew, and I were watching a *National Geographic* show that highlighted the world's quietest place on Earth—the anechoic chamber at Orfield Labs in Minneapolis, Minnesota. This place is so quiet, it can drive you nuts. The room's background noise is measured in negative decibels. Companies test their products to see how noisy they really are. Evidently, this place is so quiet, you can hear your heartbeat, your bones rubbing together, and your breathing in your lungs. This is interesting because when God speaks, it's not always with words—rather, a breath.

The Orfield Laboratory might feel a little too disorienting for us, but remember that being in the presence of God caused people in the Bible to fall face first to the ground, trembling at any sound from God with great reverence. Most of those who fall before God dare not make a sound, much less speak.

God's holy presence creates a holy hush and silence. So amazing is the presence of God that words fall short of anything divine. The Hebrew word for whisper means "silence" or "stillness. A gentle whisper from God's Spirit. And "Spirit" is the same Hebrew word for "breath."

St. John Climacus said, back in the sixth century, as he prayed throughout his life on Mt. Sinai, "The friend of silence draws near to God."[9]

That is an amazing concept—that silence creates a friendship between humans and God. In fact, I cannot think of any prophets who encountered God without drawing into the disciplines of silence and solitude.

Robert Cardinal Sarah asks, "How can man really be in the image of God? He must enter into silence. When he drapes himself in silence, as God himself dwells in a great silence, man is close to heaven, or rather, he allows God to manifest himself in him. We encounter God only in the

8. Ibid., 115.
9. St. John Climacus, *The Ladder of Divine Ascent* (London: Faber and Faber, 1959), 135.

eternal silence in which he abides."[10]

As God was working His plan for the people of Israel, He told his people in Exodus 14:14 something profound in discovering deliverance: "The Lord will fight for you; you need only to be *still.*"

Solitude is one of the very best ways to meet God. And the opposite is also true—if you want to miss God's voice, stay busy and preoccupied! Embrace ambiguity and the mystery of silence as a lifestyle, not just a weekend experience.

Silence can be a game changer. Silence has the ability to touch our souls deeply. Silence creates epiphanies that increase our self-awareness and God awareness. Silence is the great equalizer. It can show us how broken and fragile we are, and when we get quiet, we can sense how close or far away from God we really are. Silence can produce "A-ha!" moments, and as my friend, Rob, says, "The dashboard of one's soul lights up." Silence produces the small and big miracles.

Silence, however, is a means to the end, not an end in and of itself. The goal is God. Learning to get on the same frequency with God takes time. It is a process.

Thank You

From the bottom of my heart, thank you for picking up this book.

My prayer is that you feel encouraged and empowered. If I have not answered all your questions about mystery, or silence, then I feel like I succeeded in my mission! That's because if we can resolve all these issues, then our God is too small. Let God do the unveiling of the mysteries as He sees fit in His time. Sometimes, He will speak. Sometimes not. When you are trying to make sense out of life, and wondering why God feels absent, remember that God waits for you in silence.

I close with the apostle Paul's words to us all, which is my prayer for you: that you may know Christ more richly and deeply as you learn about the mystery of silence:

> "But whatever were gains to me I now consider loss for the sake of
> Christ. What is more, I consider everything a loss because of the

---

10. Robert Cardinal Sarah, *The Power of Silence*, 21.

surpassing worth of *knowing Christ Jesus my Lord,* for whose sake I have lost all things. I consider them garbage, that I may gain Christ and be found in him, not having a righteousness of my own that comes from the law, but that which is through faith in Christ—the righteousness that comes from God on the basis of faith. *I want to know Christ—yes, to know the power of his resurrection and participation in his sufferings,* becoming like him in his death."
—Philippians 3:7–10

Big Takeaway: When you feel God is absent, embrace the faith as both mystery and truth. Don't box Jesus in. Differentiate. Identify your sweet spot. Allow mystery to be just that—mystery.

Questions for Reflection

1. Can you relate to Kate Bowler's sentiment that most people who are trying to empathize with someone else's hurts and wounds really have no idea what the person is going through? How would you help someone who has doubts about why God is allowing pain and His apparent silence?
2. Of the top ten ideas from Dr. Olshine, which one do you need the most right now?
3. What are some ways to embrace the idea of mystery over certainty?
4. What steps will you take to move into more trust with God, even when things don't make any sense to you?

RESOURCES ON PRAYER, SILENCE, AND SOLITUDE

- Ruth Haley Barton, *Invitation to Solitude and Silence*, InterVarsity Press, 2010

- Laura Baber Beach, *Rhythms of Restoration: Practicing Grief on the Path of Grace: A Field Guide of Mini-Retreats for the Hurting and Those Who Help Them*, Seedbed, 2015

- Richard Foster, *Celebration of Discipline*, Harper and Row, 1998

- Emile Griffin, *Wilderness Time: A Guide for Spiritual Retreat*, RENOVARE, 1997

- Henri Nouwen, *The Way of the Heart*, Ballantine Books, 2003

- Henry Nouwen, *In the Name of Jesus*, Crossroad Publishing, 1989

- Robert Cardinal Sarah, *Power of Silence*, Ignatius Press, 2017

- Peter Scazzero, *Daily Office—Begin the Journey: Remembering God's Presence Throughout The Day*, 2008

ACKNOWLEDGMENTS

No writer ever begins or ends his or her work without tons of input and help. We need others in the best and worst ways, and this includes publishing a book you hope impacts hundreds or thousands of people.

Let me begin with my spouse, soul mate, and best friend, Rhonda Lee Olshine. We have just accomplished forty years of marriage. What an adventure it has been! Thank you. You inspire me. You make me better. Thank you for a marriage that keeps us growing with trust, love, lots of laughter, and affection. I am a grateful man. Life's journey without you would be pretty boring. Love you, honey.

To my kids, Rachel and Andrew, thank you for gracing this planet with your presence. This world is a much better place with you two. I cannot imagine life without either of you. You are both smart, funny, articulate, and a gift to the world. Thank God you look like your mom!

And to Chris Frazier for marrying up by taking my daughter's hand in marriage. Welcome to the family. And to our grandbaby, Myles, you will be getting spoiled by Poppy and Gigi.

To my mom, Tidg, and my sister, Emily, thanks for your ongoing love and support. To my extended family members, aunts, uncles, cousins, nephews, and nieces, too many to name, thanks for all you have taught me.

To Larry and Sue Wagner, Karen Grant, Julian and Loretta Goddard, Keith Wasserman, Jonathan Weibel, and Craig Garrison, who have modeled grace in the midst of hardships.

Thank you to my manuscript proofreaders. To my former editor and three decades of friendship, Dale "Dunk" Reeves. To Kara Reedy Garrison; Anne Lord Bailey; Amy Van Horn; Claire Andrews; my brother-in-law, John Weisman; my sister in-law, Valerie Weisman; lifelong buddy, Mark Rowland; Kate Oches; my fabulous editor, Libbye Morris; and author Samantha Evans. Thanks for having the perceptive eye for accuracy and content, which at times pushed me to scream out loud, but the words on the paper became more alive because of you. Thank you for spending way too much time looking over my chapters and hunting for ways to make the book flow better. Thank you from the bottom of my heart.

To Greg Johnson, my agent who is the best in the business. Thank you for your persistency to knock on some doors and shake some trees.

For my CIU family for encouraging me these past two decades to impact the world through speaking, teaching, mentoring and writing.

To my students at Columbia International University, both past and present. You have my heart. You are more than the next generation…you are the *now* generation.

To my Lord and Savior, Yeshua (Jesus), thanks for changing my life. Here's to the *Mystery of Silence!*

ABOUT THE AUTHOR

Dr. David Olshine is lead professor of Youth Ministry, Family and Culture at Columbia International University (CIU) in Columbia, South Carolina. David is a veteran youth worker, communicator to more than 2.5 million people, and the author of sixteen books. He also serves part time as teaching pastor at Sandhills Community Church. He is the founder of Youth Ministry Coaches, a consulting business that helps churches find and keep youth workers.

David married out of his league, to Rhonda, and they have two amazing kids—Rachel and Andrew; a son-in-law, Chris; and a grandson, Myles. David loves his family, reading, seafood, dark chocolate, mountains, beaches, swimming, traveling, and college football and basketball.